Beating the Odds

Beating the Odds

Poker Strategies for Leading Projects and Winning at Work

John Schroeder

Advanced Strategies Press
Atlanta, GA

Published by Advanced Strategies Press, an imprint of Advanced Strategies, Inc., 3980 DeKalb Technology Parkway, Suite 800, Atlanta, GA 30340; 770-936-4000.

Advanced Strategies, Inc. retains the rights to all copyrighted and proprietary premises and materials embedded in the text of this book.

Special discounts on bulk quantities of Advanced Strategies Press books are available to corporations, professional associations, and other organizations. For details, contact the coordinator of book sales at Advanced Strategies Press, 3980 Dekalb Technology Parkway, Suite 800, Atlanta, GA 30340; 770-936-4000; booksales@advstr.com or via website www.advancedstrategies.com/beatingtheodds.

First printing 2006

ISBN 0-9774412-0-2

LCCN 2005909124

Printed in Canada

Dedicated to my beautiful wife and daughter.

CONTENTS

Introduction – *Winning Big with Fundamentals*

Part 3 – Shuffle Up and Deal

Acknowledgements

Why Poker and Leadership?

I've wanted to write a book about project leadership for the last few years. Spending eight years as the first line of client contact for a management consulting firm enabled me to develop insights into what is working and what is not in today's environment. Talking to so many struggling people week after week helped me realize that although their project issues looked complex and unique on the surface, all the projects shared a small set of straightforward, root causes. Working with clients one-on-one, it was possible to consistently identify their underlying problems and take corrective action. If only it were possible to package this approach into something that anyone frustrated on the job could benefit from and that would be more entertaining to read than your average college textbook.

As I tried to figure out how to get the message out, I created several outlines and draft titles including *What Training for a Marathon Teaches Us about Project Discipline*, *Beer Coaster Project Management*, and my personal favorite, *Everything I Know about Project Leadership, I Learned from My Dog*. While I found it easy to frame a couple of key leadership points, each title proved to be too gimmicky, with more sizzle than substance.

Around the same time, I took up Texas hold 'em poker (along with 10 to 20 million of my closest friends). Working on projects by day and playing and reading about poker by night, a pattern started to form. While at first I was a terrible poker player, as I began to apply my consulting experiences, I began to win more at night...a lot more. Then, somewhat unexpectedly, I realized that poker analogies and examples were creeping their way into my consulting sessions. Surprisingly, these stories were able to help even my non-poker playing clients see key messages better than the illustrations I had been using for years.

I began to contemplate whether poker would be a fitting framework for my book. The final push came as I watched the World Poker Tour, and I heard announcer Mike Sexton say, "It takes a minute to learn and a lifetime to master." This phrase rang so true to both my poker and project leadership senses, that at that moment this book was born.

I wrote *Beating the Odds* to be short enough to be read on a business trip, yet substantial enough to dramatically impact success. While the take-aways provide immediate benefit, the far greater value will come from applying these strategies as you continuously improve your performance for weeks, months, and even years to come.

I hope you enjoy this book and can apply its lessons to become more successful at the table, whether it is in the poker room or the boardroom.

John Z Schroeder

INTRODUCTION

"My project is in trouble and I need some help."

Every week, I receive calls from organizations looking for help achieving project success. The conversations start off with the callers indicating that they are looking for advice, but nine times out of ten, before I have even the slightest handle on the problem, the troubled caller springs their desired solution on me - and it is rarely something simple.

They want to focus on more rigorous and scientific methods for sizing the activities of their projects and running weighted scenarios across their portfolio. They want to explore more robust and consistent use of Microsoft Project and other tools. They want to concoct a homebrew of acronyms sure to deliver success: "We need to create Centers of Excellence (COEs) to better leverage ROI, EVA, CPI, UML, TQM, and SLAs."

As the acronyms swirl through my head, I can't help but make the connection between the detailed nature of their proposed solutions and the advice many "serious" poker players dole out as they lose money week after week. They talk incessantly about the importance of being students of "advanced" poker topics such as calculating exact probabilities, memorizing starting hand charts, and applying complex game theory.

In my experience, the more people focus on so-called advanced topics, the more they neglect the basics, whether in business or poker:

> ***Some people are so busy learning the tricks of the trade that they never learn the trade.***
> - Vernon "The Preacher" Law,
> 1960 Cy Young Award Winner

1

This focus on tricks and tools is reminiscent of the tale of the Las Vegas golfer:

A weekend golfer travels to Vegas to play some poker and work on his golf game. After shooting a 120 the first day, he vows to break 100 by the end of the week. The caddy tries to convince him to take a few lessons from the golf pro and assures him he could quickly shave off 20 strokes. Does he listen? No way. Instead, he goes back to an up-scale golf store on the Strip where he plunks down a grand for the latest and greatest set of titanium irons. A few days later he returns to the course, but only two things have changed:

1. 90% of the time he hits the ball exactly the same – except now he's a little more pissed-off about it.
2. The rest of the time he still hits the ball in the wrong direction, only now he is able to hit it *much farther in the wrong direction.*

Neither of these helps his score. In fact, his score balloons to over 130.

This story illustrates why this book focuses on the fundamentals. *Beating the Odds* will help you succeed with the basic strategies that can make or break project success for anyone, beginner or expert. Yes, experts too. After all, when Tiger Woods gets in a slump, does he run out to buy a new set of clubs? Of course not. He gets together with his coach to work on the fundamentals of his swing.

Leading Projects & Winning at Work

The fundamental premise of *Beating the Odds* is that in order to breakthrough abysmal project success rates, we must change our perspective from thinking that just doing "business as usual" will work. Instead, we must adopt a project-oriented perspective focused on actively setting up a game we can win. Many individuals don't see their jobs in terms of projects to be delivered. Others fail to appreciate just how different a project-driven approach is. This combination is a primary contributor to what's wrong with today's work world.

Confusion regarding what a project is, and how one should be led, is why **organizations under perform**. It is why **half of all projects fail**. It is **why people are burned out** and **too many hate their jobs**.

Projects aren't simply about saying: "Let's do a project," or, "I'm the project leader," and then waiting for success to come to you. Projects aren't about "managing" by a constant focus on contract changes, dress codes, and time tracking.

Instead, projects are what you set up and drive when you want to get something done, and done right. Projects are what you *establish* when success depends on the output of a high performance team. Projects are what you *lead* when you don't have the authority to control your boss, your customers, and your partners.

What are the projects *Beating the Odds* applies to and how will you know them when you see them? They are everything from landing a new account, to launching a new product, to creating the perfect ad campaign. They are reorganizing your office, forming a new team, and knocking out the A#1 item on your to-do list. Projects are what you set up to deliver success in the boardroom, the conference room, and yes, even the cardroom.

Projects aren't always the fun way to play, but they are the winning way to play. And let's face it:

Life's a lot more fun when you are winning.

CHAPTER 1

The Luckiest Player I've Ever Seen:
Effectiveness Can Be Learned

- *The project failure rate continues to hover around 50%.*
  - *Wall Street & Technology*

- *Half of the decisions made in business and related organizations fail.*
  - Paul C. Nutt, *Why Decisions Fail*

- *50% of small businesses fail.*
  - U.S. Small Business Association

- *Less than 20% of the players in poker rooms breakeven over the long-term.*
  - ESPN

Beating the Odds

Achieving business success is increasingly difficult in today's chaotic, complex, and rapidly changing world. Everyone has too much to do, bosses and investors expect instant results, and customers continually raise the bar. Perhaps most challenging of all, we have virtually no authority over the people whose cooperation and hard work is necessary for us to reach our goals. With the deck seemingly stacked against us, is it surprising that over half of all projects end in failure?

Just because industry averages are poor, and just because it often feels we are dealt unlucky cards, that does not give us an excuse to accept losing performance. Effective project leaders, like successful poker players, are able to learn and implement common sense techniques to consistently beat the odds. There is no reason that you cannot become one of these successful players, winning both on the job and at your regular poker game.

Before we jump into specific techniques, we need to start by debunking two common misconceptions that lead to failure:

1. Project leadership and poker are easy.
2. Success is primarily driven by luck.

Myth 1: It Looks So Easy. It is tempting to view successful project leaders the same way we view poker professionals on television. They seem to have effortless and lucrative jobs – not really doing much of anything except sitting around, strategizing, making a few key decisions, and at the end of the day, cashing a fat paycheck. While this may seem to be the case to those on the outside, almost anyone who has held these jobs professionally will tell you that the truth is perhaps better captured by Amarillo Slim's poker adage:

It's a hard way to earn an easy living.

Why is project leadership so difficult? This book's definition of a project leader is far broader than the traditional, titled project manager leading multi-million dollar projects. The majority of professional jobs now include a significant project leadership component. Professionals must be able to leverage those around them (including those above them) to create business value for the organization.

Therefore, a project leader is anyone who:

- organizes and directs
- a group of individuals
- in achieving results
- within a definite time period
- in spite of scarce resources
- while overcoming a wide assortment of obstacles.

6

This definition may or may not be enough to make you think project leadership is more than the cushy job it is sometimes portrayed to be. So just in case, let's make our definition a little more accurate by looking at the reality of the situation.

A project leader is anyone who:
- organizes and directs
- a group of individuals
  - *many of whom are not of their choosing and out of their control;*
- in achieving results
  - *for people who can't agree on what they want, who lose interest in the effort, and whose priorities shift due to the urgency of other projects;*
- within a definite time period
  - *that is often less than what is needed and continually shrinking;*
- in spite of scarce resources
  - *that are often less than what is needed and continually shrinking;*
- while overcoming a wide assortment of other obstacles
  - *that continually grows as time goes by.*

This book isn't going to turn you into a certified project manager, and it certainly won't turn you into a professional poker player. It will teach you to apply a proven set of techniques to improve how you lead the people around you to deliver high quality project results in the type of environment described above (and it just might help your poker game as well).

Myth 2: The Importance of Luck. It's interesting how often we describe successful projects, leaders, and organizations as lucky. We have a natural tendency to look at others and credit their success to luck rather than expertise or hard work. Consider some popular, but mostly untrue, urban legends you have probably heard around the water cooler:

- Bill Gates – Lucky. Lucky an anti-monopoly government was holding back IBM. Even luckier that when IBM was selecting an operating system vendor, they were turned away from their first choice by the lead programmer's wife, who was protecting her husband's nap time. (Of course, some of this may be sour grapes.)
- Pierre Omidyar – How lucky can you get? He creates eBay as an online venue for trading Pez dispensers and it mushrooms into a billion-dollar company. (Of course in reality, this was just a PR story created after the fact.)
- Mark Cuban – Talk about lucky. First he puts himself through college giving disco lessons; then he has the world's luckiest timing, selling Broadcast.com to Yahoo for $2 billion just before the Internet boom collapses. (Of course, this was actually the *second* company he had successfully built and sold.)

Spend too much time at the water cooler and you might start to believe that these leaders would be flipping burgers at McDonald's right now if they hadn't caught that one lucky break. Then again, maybe golfer Gary Player, winner of nine majors, was more on target when he said:

The harder I practice, the luckier I get.

Even more surprising than the way we discount others' abilities is the way we tend to view our own performance. It is comical to talk with project leaders who, after defying unbelievable odds to deliver success on crazy projects, look back and honestly credit good fortune to making the difference, rather than their skill, dedication, and hard work.

Poker is much the same way. The great thing about poker, and one of the primary contributors to its exponential rise in popularity, is that it has just enough luck involved to convince weak and inexperienced players that

8

they can beat strong, experienced players. While there is certainly enough luck to swing the scales in the short run, what about the long run?

To examine the impact of luck in determining success, let's apply three tests:

- **The Consistency Test.** When you look around, can you identify project leaders (or poker players) that consistently outperform their peers week in and week out? Are these people just luckier, having been born under a good sign, or do they have abilities, natural or developed through hard work, that make them more effective?

- **The Improvement Test.** If you look back over your own experiences since you first started leading projects (or playing poker), has your performance improved? If so, have you grown luckier, or have you developed your skill sets, strategies, and experiences?

- **The Bet Your Life Test.** If twelve months from now your life were to depend on it, do you think you could significantly improve at poker? At project leadership? Would you spend your time stock-piling rabbit's feet, four leaf clovers, and Hawaiian idols? Or, would you learn and practice techniques for improving your performance?

If you answered yes to any of these questions, then poker and project leadership must be about more than luck. While there is undoubtedly some good luck and bad luck in everything we do, luck balances out in the long run. Therefore, long-term success requires developing strategies for consistently beating the odds. To quote management guru, Peter Drucker:

Effectiveness can be learned.

A Framework for Effectiveness

When you get dealt a great hand, there are lots of ways to win and lots of ideas and decisions to which you can credit success. When I worked at Intel, people credited much of Intel's success to an open door culture evidenced by the fact that everyone up to the CEO had a cubicle, and there were no offices. However, since my friends that worked at Microsoft credited Microsoft's success to the fact that everyone had an office and there were no cubicles, I began to suspect that:

Just because you were successful - not everything you decided, did, or put in place was the key to success.

Beating the Odds provides a roadmap for what to do not only when you are dealt great cards but also what to do when you are dealt difficult ones. In Texas hold 'em, you can be dealt 1,326 different combinations of down cards. Of these, roughly five percent are truly strong starting hands. Another fifteen percent may have potential, but the vast majority, the other eighty percent, don't have any real chance of delivering positive returns over the long-term.

Projects tend to feel the same way. If you look at the activities on your plate, you are lucky if you have anything that resembles a pair of aces. You probably have a few items that have the strength of an ace-queen or ace-jack, but most projects are true long shots. The *Beating the Odds* approach is designed to help you turn these long shots into projects you can win and then play them to success.

The following poker chip illustrates the seven elements required for project success.

The four elements that you must put in place to have a game you can win are:
1. **Specified Results** – to drive decision making.
2. **Adaptable Plans** – that are modified according to changing circumstances.
3. **Dedicated Resources** – to carry out the plan and achieve the results.
4. **Sufficient Time Span** – enough to aggressively meet the needs of the situation.

Once you have ensured these four core elements are in place, is success guaranteed? Not at all – but what you will have is a legitimate shot at success because you now hold a strong hand. To actually deliver success then requires you to have:
5. **A Focus on People** – poker is a game of people and so is leadership.
6. **Discipline** – actually doing what you know needs to be done.
7. **Courage** – to make the calls (or folds) that are difficult, unpopular, and sometimes scary.

11

BEATING THE ODDS

PART 1

Setting Up a Game You Can Win

Every battle is won before it is ever fought.
– Sun Tzu, *The Art of War*

BEATING THE ODDS

CHAPTER 2

The "All-In Test":
Specified Results Must Drive Your Decisions

One of the most influential writers on effectiveness, Stephen Covey, has a famous habit:

Begin with the end in mind.

Poker legend Doyle Brunson puts it a little more bluntly:

A man needs a motive to play poker.
For me, it's money.

It seems both of these experts would agree that the first step in setting up a game you can win is to decide what it means to "win". What are the ends, the specified results, the final measures of success that should guide us when playing poker?

- Making money?
- Being social?
- Winning hands?
- Relaxing?
- Receiving an adrenaline rush?
- Getting a night out?

While many people feel the "right" response is to take Doyle Brunson's stance and insist, "I play poker to make money," there is actually no inherently right or wrong answer to this question. In fact, if the majority of poker players were to divide the amount of money they earned at poker by their time spent, they would quickly realize either their desired end result is not really winning money; or, if they really are in need of money, they would probably be better off moonlighting at the local coffee shop than playing poker.

So, if it is not money that defines the ends, what is it? As a poker player, you should take the time to think about and specify the results you are seeking in playing the game. In other words, what are your primary intentions for playing that you will use to judge whether or not you have been successful.

Why is this analysis so critical?

**Because the ends will dictate
how you play in various situations.**

For instance, consider the following example from Texas hold'em:

Five Community Cards

You

Your Opponent

(While you don't need to play poker to get value from this book, to best understand the examples you may want to review the rules of Texas hold 'em in the Appendix.)

In this example, you currently have a nothing hand. You hold 2-3, while the community cards shared by you and you opponent are A-K-J-4, which don't improve your hand. The only card that could help you is a 5, since it would give you a straight (A-2-3-4-5). Therefore, your chance of having the better hand after the final card is revealed is less than one in ten. Your opponent places a huge bet. What do you do?

If your primary end is making money, you cannot call this bet. I repeat, you *cannot* call this bet. In the long run, "chasing the straight" will lose you far more money than it will ever win.

However, if your primary ends include an adrenaline rush and/or beating this particular opponent, maybe you should go ahead and call. While you will still probably lose, if you do get your 5 you will have a great rush, a great win over your rival, and something fun to talk about over the next few minutes, days, or even weeks. *"You should have seen his face when he saw that I spiked a 5 on the river!"*

As poker players, we must know our ends, the specified results we are seeking, because it will dictate how we play the game. While ideally we would like to have it all - money, fun, excitement, drinks, jokes, and relaxation - and even though all of these are often interconnected, we want to make sure we stay focused on what we *primarily* are trying to accomplish. Not only do we want to begin with the end in mind, but we also want to use those specified results as a constant reminder of why we are playing and use them to drive our decision making as we choose to fold, call, or raise. Further, these same results should drive our pre-game decisions as we look at:

- Who should we play with - friends, enemies, strangers?
- What game should we play - hold 'em, Omaha, queen follow the queen, guts?
- Where should we play - home, a friend's house, online, the local cardroom, Vegas?
- How much money should we play for?
- When should we quit?

Likewise, as project leaders, we must first know our ends and then let those specified results dictate the decisions we make and actions we take. As with poker, there are multiple ends that can be used to signify project success. Popular answers to the question, "How will we measure project success?" include:

- Being on time and on budget.
- Delivering a product or service.
- Completing all tasks.
- Providing all specified functionality.
- Surviving and not getting fired.

The message is not that any of these answers are inherently good or bad. Rather, it is important to know what the primary drivers are because they will determine how you should proceed. Suppose, for example, your next project is to lead a team in making improvements to your company's website. The chart below shows how different desired results might naturally culminate in different products.

Desired Result	Resulting Website
Promote your organization's products and services to potential new customers.	A static online brochure.
Build relationships with your existing and most valued customers.	An interactive forum for communications.
Enhance internal efficiency by improving the ability to schedule activities.	An online calendar system.

To take it a step further, suppose your next project is to set up and run a restaurant. Looking at the following list, match the probable restaurant that would emerge depending on the desired end result.

Desired Result	Resulting Restaurant
1. Make your *fortune* by building a franchising empire.	a. Hip, five star restaurant
2. Own and work in the *cozy atmosphere* you have always dreamed of.	b. Fast food shop
3. Achieve *prestige* as a world-class restaurateur.	c. Quaint, sidewalk café

Even in this simplistic example, there are at least two major reasons why starting with the end in mind is critically important in projects:

1. **Avoiding Buyer's Remorse** - You need to figure out your specified results up front so the sponsors, those paying for the project, don't end up with something they don't want, e.g. you deliver a five star restaurant when they really wanted a sidewalk café. Now they are further from their actual goal because they are stuck with high dollar people, property, and equipment.

2. **Aligning Action without Micro-managing** - There are literally thousands of decisions that will need to be made to successfully complete this project. You want your team to make consistent decisions and take consistent actions. No one wants, or has time for, micro-management so it is critical that the team is making decisions based on a consistent, documented vision of the specified results rather than reverting to their individual preferences and notions. The last thing you can afford is to have your HR person out hiring a world renowned chef, while your operations person celebrates saving $5,000 by getting a great deal on 50,000 plastic sporks.

In the buyer's remorse scenario, the restaurant might be "successfully" delivered on time and on budget but in reality it is a failure because it does not provide ongoing satisfaction to the sponsors. In the second scenario, because the actions and decisions are in conflict, the project is likely to suffer delays, budget overruns, and even cancellation.

Industry statistics on information technology (IT) project success rates, one of the most widely studied types of projects, are not encouraging:

- "61% of the projects were deemed to have failed."
  – KPMG Canada Survey

- "While most companies got their software to run, only 35% were satisfied with the ROI."
  – Information Week
- "Morgan Stanley estimates that U.S. companies threw away $130 billion in the past two years on unneeded software and other technology."
  – USA Today

Ken Brame, CIO of AutoZone, sums up IT's accomplishments as follows:

Only in baseball do we reward these kinds of averages and accept that we are only going to get a hit once out of every three trips to the plate.

It is tempting and easy to pick on technologists because technology failures are so often highly visible. So what about the rest of us? Do we really deliver business results more consistently than the folks in IT?

- "More than half of all corporate mergers destroy shareholdervalue." – *The Economist*
- "Success with outsourcing mirrors that of the divorce rate; one in five deals ends within a year, and 50% of all deals end in five years."
  - Information Week
- "Only 10 percent of the books published earn out their advances. Nine out of ten books fail!"
  - Random House

How Do We Decide on Our Specified Results?
And Who Is "We" Exactly?
With poker players, like project leaders, the lack of specified results often comes down to an unwillingness to honestly prioritize. In poker:

- Playing loose is more fun - but playing tight wins more money.
- Drinking is more fun - but staying sober wins more money.
- Staying up and out is more fun - but going home to bed saves more money.

21

- Playing with your friends is more fun - but playing suckers brings in more money.

As poker players, we must manage our scarce resources – there is only so much time and money we can spend on poker. Therefore, we need to prioritize what we most want out of this endeavor *including* deciding what desirable things we are willing to sacrifice to get there. The following chart identifies some common scenarios in terms of priority results and the things we want but are willing to sacrifice for our priorities:

Priority Results	To Reach These I Am...
Blowing Off Steam Getting your mind off work and relaxing.	Willing to sacrifice winning money.
Winning Money	Willing to sacrifice the excitement of playing loose, drinking beer, and playing with good friends.
Catching up with Friends Seeing people you know and enjoy.	Willing to sacrifice an opportunity to move to a different table and play against drunk tourists for easy money.
Building Excitement Putting some adrenaline in your life.	Willing to sacrifice playing with friends to take a seat at the no-limit table filled with high rollers.

This chart may seem to imply that you can't have fun and win money, which is not necessarily the case. However, there are often a few key decisions before and during play that will test your fun versus money priorities. One test for determining where your poker priorities lie in terms of fun versus money is to consider your response when asked the question: Who is playing this week? If you tend to think or say, I am playing *with* Sandy, Todd, and BC, rather than I am playing *against* Sandy, Todd, and BC, it is less likely that your primary driver is money.

Just as with poker players, project leaders often have a hard time prioritizing the specified results and identifying what they are willing to sacrifice for those results. On projects:

- Focusing on getting the work completed on time and on budget is safer for your career – but fighting the battles to ensure things are done right has greater potential for results.
- Working on what's sexy (new technology, new buzz words, new Super Bowl ads, etc.) is more fun – but taking care of business by completing mundane, essential tasks has a much higher payback.
- Taking a revolutionary approach is more exciting – but an evolutionary approach is safer.
- Thinking "if we build it, they will come" is easier – but a collaborative, customer-centric approach is more likely to deliver sustained business results.

This is not a black or white, right or wrong, type of question. While we may want all these things, given the scarcity of time, money, and other resources, we must ask the question: what are we willing to sacrifice when push comes to shove to reach the desired results?

Satisfying Your Sponsors

Throughout the previous examples, it is stressed that there are no inherently right or wrong choices, just decisions to be made so that everyone is aligned in their efforts and we don't lose focus on our priorities. In many cases, this is an oversimplification. Before we can begin to specify our results, we must first identify who is "bankrolling" or "sponsoring" the effort and make sure they are the ones specifying the results. Take a look at the following three pictures:

In case you can't tell, the guy on the left with the tie around his head is "Single Guy." When he is playing poker, he is playing with *his* money. This is good news for his opponents, since he freely parts with his money. (Although when playing him you should be cautious since he does not have to consider anyone but himself when he risks all his chips calling your bluff.)

The second guy used to be single guy playing with his own money but now he is "Married Guy" playing with *their* money – or as many have pointed out to me - *her* money.

The third guy on the right (not pictured) has a new daughter. While up to this point he may have thought he was playing with his money, now there is no doubt that he is playing with *her* money.

So what does this mean for "New Dad"? It is no longer enough for him to figure out his priorities. He has to figure out what the owners of the money are willing to invest in. Before, his priorities might have been:

- Specified Result: Blowing off a lot of steam.
- Willing to Sacrifice: A lot of money and a lot of time.

Now that his daughter is effectively bankrolling him, his priorities might become:

- Specified Result: Blowing off some steam and breaking even.
- Willing to Sacrifice: The potential for a big adrenaline rush and staying out all night.

Appropriate strategies would include: playing tight instead of loose, playing once a week instead of all the time, and playing low-limit instead of no-limit.

To see how this plays out, let's return to our earlier example of chasing the straight:

You   **Your Opponent**

Since the desired end results must dictate a player's decisions, while Single Guy might be "right" in chasing the straight, hoping for that miracle card and getting that rush, New Dad has to fold. He no longer can continue to throw in money from his daughter's college fund on what he mathematically knows is a losing bet.

As project leaders, we must constantly remind ourselves and our team whose money we are playing with. At work, it is highly unlikely that we are Single Guy playing with our own bankroll. In most cases, we are definitely NOT playing with our own money. Even if it is our budget and our project, that does not make it our money. It is the stockholders, taxpayers, owners, etc. who are staking us with the money, people, and other resources with which we are working.

What does this mean? When you are bankrolled in poker it means you are no longer playing to have fun; you are playing to earn a return on the sponsor's investment. In project leadership, it means that ends such as:

- Coming in on time and on budget
- Delivering a product or service
- Building your resume
- Having fun

are **_NOT_** enough.

The only acceptable ends for projects bankrolled with other people's money is:

Delivering the sponsor's specified business results.

No matter how on-time or on-budget your project is, if it does not create the desired business value it cannot be called a success. An accomplishment? Sure. A heroic effort? Probably. But not a success. One of the most widely quoted ways for defining project success is given below:

A project is a temporary endeavor
undertaken to create a _unique product or service_.
- Project Management Institute, *PMBOK Guide*

While this is true enough, when you are being bankrolled by stockholders or taxpayers you must hold yourself to an even higher standard in defining your projects:

Project leadership is the marshaling of resources to produce a _specified set of business outcomes_.

Why? Because it is not _your_ bankroll. It might help if someone from accounting (or the legislature) periodically dressed up as Tony Soprano and met with project leaders to explain bankrolling in poker terms: "Look, I am not bankrolling you to *play* poker, I am staking you to *make* money. In other words, you are not being paid to *lead* a project, you are being paid to *create value* for this organization."

Admittedly, it can be difficult to shift your thinking away from the product or service your sponsor has requested to the business results they desire. Often, this is because the business results are not crystal clear in your sponsor's head. Therefore, it would be impossible to be clear in yours, let alone on a piece of paper you both agree to. To make matters worse, when there are multiple sponsors, they may agree on the product or solution but disagree on the desired business results and not even know it.

A few years ago, I was involved with a project at a very large manufacturing firm where they had purchased a $1 million piece of equipment to match the color of materials. After a few weeks, their implementation project was in disarray. Process consultants were brought in to identify the root cause of the problem. Once discovered, the problem was straight forward enough. While everyone agreed the new piece of equipment was a product that was needed, one part of the implementation team thought the goal was to speed the time of delivery by replacing the laborious manual color matching process. The other half of the team thought the primary goal was to improve quality and reduce defects by performing a quality control double-check after the manual process was completed. The first group thought the machine needed to be integrated into the front of the process, and the second group, in the back of the process. They kept tripping over each other as they continually reconfigured the line.

This company's problem, confusion over how to implement a solution, stemmed from a deeper cause: differing visions of the outcomes to be delivered from this investment. An efficient way to help prevent this type of confusion over a project's goals is to use:

The Currency of Your Project Test. For the project, ask the question, "Why are we doing this, in terms of the one currency that will most be used to judge successful business results?"

For instance, for tonight's poker game will you judge success in the currency of:

- Money won?
- Profit earned (money won less pizza, beer, and gas expenses)?

- Fun had?
- Excitement generated?
- Beer consumed?

For the color matching example, the question was how would they judge the success of integrating the new machine into the manufacturing process? In the currency of:

- Time shaved off the delivery cycle?
- Defects eliminated?
- Labor reduced?

For another example, let's look at a typical project goal: create a website that improves customer service efficiency. Based on this charge, one could easily assume at least three separate and potentially conflicting currencies for measuring success. Therefore, as project leaders, we must work with our sponsors to ensure we have precisely and concisely specified which of the following currencies we are primarily seeking. Is it:

- Cost efficiency – measured by how much we lower the organization's *cost* of providing customer service.
- Time efficiency - measured by how much we reduce *response time* to customer requests.
- Stress efficiency - measured by how much we reduce *frustrations* of our customer service representatives and customers.
- Or something else?

Take a moment to think about how one of your current projects is defined. How would you describe the currency of project success? Is there agreement regarding the desirable things you are willing to sacrifice to reach those results?

A second test for ensuring project leaders, project sponsors, and project team members have a consistent target is to examine the results in terms of *outputs* versus *outcomes*. An output is generally defined as something produced or manufactured, while an outcome is the *business impact* of the outputs. Looking at how you just defined your project's success, was it in terms of an output or an outcome? Defining success in terms of outcomes is preferable to ensure a laser-like focus on generating business value.

Once you have identified the specified results in terms of outcomes and expressed them in the appropriate project currency, the third and final test to determine if you are truly after business value is:

The All-In Test. Meet with the people who are paying for the project and say to them: "The goal of this project is to deliver the following outcomes: X, Y, & Z."

- If their response is, "I'm all-in" (or if they are not poker players, "Bingo"), you are probably focused on desired business results expressed in terms of outcomes and described with the appropriate project currency.
- If, on the other hand, their response is, "Why are we doing that again?" you are at serious risk of being focused on something other than business results, and you need to explore with them the anticipated value to be delivered.

The All-In Test can help eliminate two of the primary causes of project failure. Project leaders and teams that focus solely on creating a "product or service" (a.k.a. outputs) often deliver on-time solutions that are rarely or never used. A lack of consensus among sponsors, leaders, and team members on the desired business results leads to confusion, conflict, and cancellation.

As a leader,

1. If you are being bankrolled by stockholders or taxpayers, the end result must be to *create business value*.
2. Make sure to specify desired business value:
   - Identify the *currency* of the project.
   - Make sure it ties to *outcomes*, not just outputs.

- To be sure you have it right, document your understanding of the desired business value and put it to the *All-In Test* with the sponsors.
- Once you are in agreement, *communicate* the specified results to the entire team.

3. Ensure everyone is using the specified results to dictate how they make decisions and take action throughout the project.

You do not need any scientific formulas or industrial strength tools to ensure your project is headed in the right direction. A post-it note or cocktail napkin will do as long as it has the following information:

Napkin Specified End Results Template

Project Name: _____

Desired Results – The Ends We Are After:
(In terms of outcomes and expressed with the project currency)

_____

_____

Who is Bankrolling the Effort:_____

Are They All-In? ( ) Yes   ( ) No

CHAPTER 3

Know When to Hold 'Em:
The Necessity of Adaptable Plans

In politics, nothing happens by accident.
If it happens, you can bet it was planned that way.
- Franklin D. Roosevelt

Successful project leadership and successful poker playing require two separate but equally important components: knowing where you are going, and knowing how you will get there.

Chapter 2 focused on: defining efforts in terms of desired end results so there is a consistent, documented image of where the project is going, and ensuring that the destination delivers value to the sponsors.

This chapter focuses on creating an adaptable plan for how to get there. Assuming you have an agreed to end in mind – for instance traveling with a team from Pensacola to Key West – the next question is, how do you work together to get there? Will you drive, power boat, sail, or fly? If you decide to sail, are you going to:

- Work together for 12 hour shifts then rest, or split into three shifts and sail 24-7?
- Stay close to shore or can you cut across the Gulf?
- Wait a couple of days until the wind picks up or leave now?

The above example may sound like Project Planning 101, but it will help illustrate what poker strategy has to teach us about project planning. First, let's take a look at one of the most widely accepted definitions of a project plan:

> A *formal, approved* document used to *guide*
> project *execution* and *control.*
> Project Management Institute, *PMBOK Guide*

As project leaders, doesn't this sound perfect? Isn't this what we all want? A formal document that has been approved at the highest levels that spells out marching orders you can execute and use to control the troops. As you boat to Key West in a scull, you can stand as the coxswain shouting, "Stroke! Stroke! Stroke! Now the Left! Now the Right! Again!" All this based on the plan, the formally approved plan. Glorious!

This sounds great in theory, but to quote computer scientist Jan L. A. van de Snepscheut: "In theory, there is no difference between theory and practice. But, in practice, there is." *Beating the Odds,* inspired by the American Management Association's characterization of an objective, proposes a slightly different definition for what a project plan represents. You should know that when this definition is presented, it is almost always met with a combination of confusion, resistance, and open hostility. One executive went so far as to say, and I quote, "ARE YOU

INSANE?" In fact, at one training session, someone disliked this definition so much that when it was presented,
they actually pulled the fire alarm! (Although my col-
leagues try to convince me it was only a coincidence.) So
what is the inflammatory definition?

**A project plan is a <u>temporary</u>,
<u>imprecise</u> model
of a desired future process
whose successful execution
can be reasonably believed to be likely,
but is <u>not certain</u>.**

Not that you would have missed them, but I under-
lined the key phrases that seem to generate most of the
hostility:
- <u>Temporary</u>
- <u>Imprecise</u>
- <u>Not Certain</u>

What is the end result that I am after when using this
more fluid definition of a project plan?
- To appear clever?
- To create something to trademark and sell?
- To be difficult?

None of the above. The outcome I am after is to
help project leaders improve their project success rates.
Over the years, the debate between these two definitions of project plans has been one of the most live-
ly and heated of my consulting career. Fortunately,
poker has provided me with an example that has
helped illustrate some of the validity in our more
"mushy" definition of a project plan.

Example: Beating the Vault. You are playing poker
heads-up (a.k.a. one-on-one) against a long time foe who
you have nicknamed "the Vault." She is a very good player, and you call her the Vault because money goes in but it
never comes back out. She never bluffs and never plays
with something less than a probable sure thing.

The initial two cards are dealt:

You   **The Vault**

Finally, after weeks of play you at last have her where you want her. You have two aces, pocket rockets, a pair of bullets, American Airlines, the Battleship Lorenzen - whatever you care to call them – the best possible starting hand in Texas hold 'em. In fact, you realize that heads-up you will win 80% of the time from this starting hand. So what do you do?

You know you need a game plan, and you know it should have two components:

1. What is the end I have in mind for this hand?
2. How am I going to get there?

Your natural reaction to the first question is simple enough. My desired result is to: <u>Win this hand.</u> But when you ask yourself: "what are the outcomes and currency of this project?" you realize it is not the amount of *hands* you win that you care about, but rather the amount of *money* you win that represents the result you are after. So, you change your desired end result to read: Take as much of the Vault's *money* as possible.

With the outcome clearly specified, the next step is to transform this end result into a plan that will enable you to accomplish your goal. You develop a plan to place a large bet so she will fold, and you will win the hand. You quickly realize this would be the wrong move since the outcome and currency you are after is winning money, not winning hands. Therefore, you adjust and come up with a three-step plan:

1. Place a medium sized bet up front.
2. Wait for her call.
3. Push all of your money in after the flop.

Remembering that you are not playing with your money (strangely your poker game has been federally funded), and that it is a so-called "best practice" to have a plan that is *a **formal**, **approved** document*, you go off to get the signature of the President. You use the All-In Test saying, "The goal of this project is to win as much of the Vault's money as possible, and you should know I have pocket rockets which will win 80% of the time." The President says, "I'm all-in," and signs off on your plan to place a medium sized bet upfront and then to push all of the taxpayer money in after the flop.

Because you are playing with so much taxpayer money, you hire a consultant to help you push all this cash into the pot after the flop (for their standard two percent). You sign a contract and get their company CEO to sign off on it. Your specified results and plan read as follows:

Specified Results and Plan

Desired Result:
Take as much of the Vault's money as possible.

Project Currency: Money won

Project Plan:
        Step 1: Place a medium sized bet.
        Step 2: Wait for her call.
        Step 3: After the flop, push all of the money in.

Approvals:

El Presidente	President of the U.S.A.
Joey Rocko	President of Moose & Rocko Consulting
<your name here>	Project Leader

You get back to the table, double check to make sure you still have your pair of bullets, and place your medium sized bet. The Vault calls your bet. You see the flop:

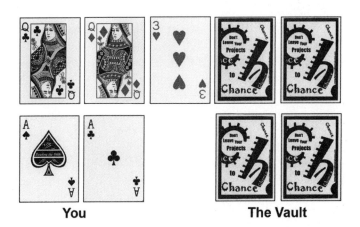

You   **The Vault**

As you digest the cards, the Vault makes a strong bet. What do you do? Your first reaction is: I have a formal, approved document used to guide project execution and control that is signed by the President and includes a contract with a consulting firm. It clearly states:

Project Plan:
    ~~Step 1: Place a medium-sized bet.~~ Done
    ~~Step 2: Wait for her call.~~ Done
    Step 3: After the flop, push all of the money in.

So, you push all of the taxpayers' money in – Right? Before you answer, let's analyze the situation with what you now know:
- The Vault never bets unless she has a winning hand.
- That means at least one of her cards is probably a queen, giving her three queens.
- Therefore, while your initial chances of winning were ~80%, your odds have now fallen to less than 10%, since only a third ace can save you.

36

If you were Single Guy playing poker with your money in New Orleans, it doesn't matter; you can blindly follow the plan. But you are not Single Guy and this is not Fat Tuesday. You feel an aching in your gut that tells you following the formal, approved plan is going to throw away a lot of the taxpayers' money.

Maybe the better strategy is to treat your plan as <u>temporary</u> and <u>imprecise</u>. Now that you are into the project and have learned more information, you could iterate the plan to include your new understanding of the situation. Instead of: push all of the money in, maybe your next step should be to... (dread) fold.

Before you can throw your cards away, you hear your boss' voice in your head, "Why did we create a plan and get it signed by the President if you were going to change it!?! Do you know what kind of hell I am going to catch for this! You know how he feels about flip-floppers." So, maybe rather than face that wrath, you should just go ahead and push all of the taxpayers' money into the pot.

The good news/bad news here is that you simply cannot, I repeat cannot, throw their money away. As a project leader, your desired end result is <u>not</u> to:

- Follow the plan.
- Make your boss happy.
- Do what is easy.

Your end is to create business value. This dictates that the best move to make is folding, rather than throwing the money away.

One of the primary causes of poker losses is the unwillingness of players to adjust their plan when the situation calls for it. Go to any cardroom and you can see it happen over and over and over again. The player starts with a strong hand. Once the dealer reveals dangerous cards and their opponents place scary bets, they realize it's a lost cause. Yet, they continue to bet and lose a huge pot. Why? They will admit, "I knew I was in trouble but I just couldn't fold this hand. My mind was made up."

Gerald Weinberg, in *The Secrets of Consulting*, sums it up nicely:

> *It may look like a crisis but it is only the end of an illusion.*

When the Vault turns over her three queens to beat your two aces to take all the money, it is not a crisis, it is not even a surprise, it is simply the end of an illusion.

Projects are the same way. It is tempting to treat your plan as fixed and unchangeable, to put your head down and charge ahead even though in your heart you know you will not be able to break through the wall that has popped up in your path. Then, once you hit the wall, it is easy to say, "We are now having a crisis on our project."

The more difficult, but in the long-term more successful approach, is to be **adaptable** in project planning. The term adapt means *to make modifications according to changing circumstances.*

No doubt it is critical to create a baseline plan that reflects what you know at the outset. It is equally as critical to adapt as you learn more information. Why are projects often late and over-budget?

1. We stick to a map that no longer matches the terrain.
2. We do not adequately plan for the obstacles that may pop up.
3. We do not adjust the plan once obstacles do pop up.
4. We fail to capitalize on the opportunities that arise. After all, obstacles will slow us down, so if we don't capitalize on the opportunities, how will we ever catch up?

So why should we think of plans as:

<u>**Temporary**</u>,
<u>**imprecise**</u> **models**
of a desired future process
whose successful execution
can be reasonably believed to be likely,
but is <u>not certain</u>?

Because the world is complex, chaotic, and changing faster every day. Successful project leaders are nimble enough and confident enough to make changes, rather than throwing money away on an illusion they know will no longer work.

It is this need for adaptation that led General Dwight Eisenhower to coin the phrase:

Plans are useless but planning is essential.

And for Kenny Rogers to sing:

You've got to know when to hold 'em,
know when to fold 'em, know when to walk away
and know when to run.[1]

---

[1]"The Gambler," written by Don Schlitz.

BEATING THE ODDS

CHAPTER 4

Jacks or Better:
Projects Require Dedicated Resources

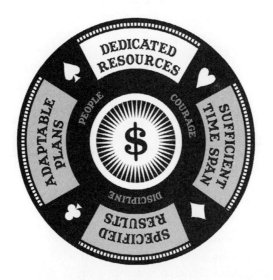

Unless commitment is made, there are only
promises and hopes; but no plans.
- Peter Drucker

At some point, a threshold must be crossed if an idea is to transition out of the dream world and into reality. For both poker and projects, this defining moment occurs when you ante up and dedicate serious resources to the effort.

A great way to see the distinction between illusion and reality is to go online and watch some of the "free poker schools". On these sites, where people play with fake money, you will quickly realize that what looks and sounds like poker is anything but the real thing. The difference? Commitment of resources. After all, when there is zero money on the line, no real time investment required, and players don't even have to use their real names, is it any wonder that these games are little more than a bunch of people going all-in every other hand? Even if you wanted to pretend the money was real in order to practice and improve your game, the lack of resource commitment from the other participants at the table makes learning, not to mention fun, nearly impossible.

Similarly, if you walk into most organizations and ask people to list all of the projects that they are involved in, or supposed to be involved in, it is not uncommon for them to name five, ten, fifteen, or even more projects, all on top of their regular workload. Examine any one of these efforts on paper, and it may look and feel like a real project complete with goals, an identified sponsor, status reports, code name, and a beautiful Gantt chart showing the proposed schedule and dependencies. However, like the free poker schools, the image can be deceiving because the lack of truly committed resources makes it more of a mirage than a reality.

Part of the reason this situation occurs is because of the spontaneous and emotional way in which projects tend to get launched in many organizations. First, someone comes up with a great idea for what the organization needs that promises to address a longstanding pain or capitalize on the latest and greatest opportunity. Then, people get excited and want to help, so they volunteer themselves or their staff (or they get volunteered). They sign up without considering what they can realistically take off their already overloaded plate to make room for this new project. On paper, and even through the first few meetings, the new effort looks fully staffed and funded. However, once the honeymoon period wears off and the effort must compete with other high priority projects, daily firefighting, people's real jobs, and life outside work, there is often nothing left to fuel these great ideas and grand plans.

In many organizations, these "ghost town" efforts have become so prevalent that they have developed their own nicknames: unfunded mandates, parking lot initiatives, C-priorities, side-items, phase next, wish list, etc.

Jacks or Better to Open

In one variation of five-card draw there is a rule called "Jacks or Better to Open". In this game, after the initial cards are dealt, if you don't have at least a pair of jacks you cannot open the betting. If no one has a strong starting hand, all of the hands are mucked (given back to the dealer) and the players must move on to the next hand. There are no exceptions. No matter how much you want to play your hand, if it isn't at least a pair of jacks you cannot open the betting – period.

It is time for this rule to make the leap from the poker room to the conference room and be applied by organizations each and every time a project is launched. After a project is initiated (i.e. the desired end results are agreed to and the initial plan is created) a checkpoint should be taken to apply the following test.

The Jacks or Better Test. Given the project's scope and plan, ask: "Does it have the dedicated resources needed for success?" If not, the participants must either:

1. Fold it. Move onto something that has a more realistic chance at success; or
2. Sound the alarm. Immediately acquire the necessary resources to have a shot at winning.

In Texas hold 'em, because all players share the same five community cards, most of the time the hand that starts the strongest will stay the strongest. Likewise, hands that start weak usually stay weak. Similarly, on projects, those that start with a great deal of momentum and strong resource commitments fare far better than those that "limp in" with less than the necessary resources.

How can you make the Jacks or Better rule a reality in your business or agency? If you are a CEO, CIO, or other executive in charge of overseeing projects, you can put processes and culture in place to review the launching and prioritizing of projects, including the dedication of resources.

As a C-level executive, you would probably go into shock if your line managers and staff started hiring people off-the-cuff, acquiring new facilities on their own, or making significant investments in capital equipment without some kind of formal planning process. Yet, somehow it is acceptable for people to launch projects that fly under the radar and whose price tag can quickly sneak up on the organization.

What does it cost when someone comes up with a bright idea that sounds great and will take:

- One lead person eight weeks;
- Five support people four weeks; and
- Another ten internal customers one week?

Added up, this scenario equates to 1520 hours. Assuming the organization estimates its cost of labor at ~$70/hour (including overhead), someone has just committed over $100,000 to undertake this project! At the same time, they probably put other $100,000 plus efforts at risk by pillaging some of those projects' resources.

Jacks or Better for the Rest of Us

For those of us responsible for day-to-day delivery of projects, the situation can be even more difficult. Whether our job is seen as leading formal projects or just completing major items on a to-do list, we face two overlapping challenges.

First, it is easy to become emotionally invested in the successful delivery of projects. You can see this parental-like attachment in how people talk about efforts, calling them "my project" even when someone else pays for them and is the prime beneficiary of the outcomes. (Imagine if you were having a house built and the architect started running around calling it *his* house; you would pretty quickly correct him that it is *your* house.) Once this emotional bond has formed, it becomes difficult for project leaders to be honest with themselves about their lack of dedicated resources, to resist over committing as to what can be realistically accomplished, and to restrain from promising heroics to overcome their projects' shortcomings and resource limitations.

Second, too many organizational cultures seem to believe that a person speaking up to say they don't have the resources needed to be successful is a sign of weakness and ineffectiveness. For those organizations, it is crucial to remember:

The gutsiest move in poker is not bluffing.
What really takes guts is folding a hand that
started out looking like a sure winner,
so that you may survive to fight another day.

To overcome parental-like bias and anti-folding cultures, it helps to enlist the assistance of a well-respected peer to do an unbiased review of your project's resources. An outsider is often a lot more realistic than those caught up in the emotional excitement of the project. They also have a lot less to lose by saying, "This project needs more help."

How do these peer reviews work? First, pick someone within your company but outside the project who you and others respect and who can give an accurate assessment of whether the project's resources are adequate. Second, ask them to examine the project's staffing and to dig below what is reflected on paper to get a true estimate of whether the project is:

- The best possible starting hand (A-A).
- A probable winner (J-J).
- Borderline realistic - has a chance but will need a lot of luck (Q-10).
- A long shot (Q-2).
- Something they would simply not bet on (7-2).

Conduct peer reviews not only as the project is launched, but also periodically throughout the project's lifecycle to make sure resources aren't being slowly siphoned off. Projects, like poker, are games of incomplete information; therefore, you must review your status after every card is turned. If at any time you or the reviewer feels that you have less than a probable winner, you must take action.

Peer reviews can be formal or informal, but must be written and should contain at least the following minimal set of information:

Napkin Resource Assessment

Project Name:_____

Reviewer:_____

Reviewing the specified results, project plan, and staffing, the current status is as follows:

Each key person assigned to this project:	Red	Yellow	Green
• Has the required knowledge and skills.	O	O	O
• Is available for the time promised.	O	O	O
• Will work well with the team and other stakeholders.	O	O	O

The biggest challenges and obstacles for this project are:

(1): _____

(2): _____

(3): _____

	Red	Yellow	Green
Based on the staffing and other resources, the project is well positioned to overcome the challenges and deliver the specified results.	O	O	O

Leveraging the Peer Review Results

As the project leader, it may not be politically feasible to say, "I don't think we have the resources for success." However, it may be possible to say, "I felt that our project was at risk of having insufficient resources, so I took it upon myself to seek a second opinion from Amy, one of our senior project managers based in Atlanta. Her assessment is that we are seriously under staffed, under supported, and under funded in these specific key areas. I agree and want to take action on this. What can we do?"

Always remember, in poker there is a term for the situation where a bet is placed without a foundation of solid resources (i.e. good cards) – it's called a bluff. While the occasional well-placed poker bluff can be very valuable, bluffing needs to be the rare exception rather than the rule. There is an apt saying regarding the pushing of all of your chips in the pot when you don't have the cards:

All-in bluffs work every time - except the last time.

While you may get away with bluffing your way through a project for awhile, eventually, reality is going to look you up and see that you don't have what is necessary to take down the pot.

Projects Dying on the Vine

Adequately dedicating resources requires not only a process for staffing projects at launch, but also a rigorous approach for canceling projects. A good paradigm to follow is that of the experienced gardener. Periodically, gardeners take the time to prune back all of a plant's branches and flowers that are unhealthy or unneeded. Why is that? Even though the branches are sick, they still consume some of the plant's nutrients and water, robbing these precious resources from healthy areas, and thus, denying them the full resources needed to thrive.

Rarely do organizations have a good process for pruning projects. Instead, they often have a myriad of projects more or less dying on the vine, as portrayed in the following scenario.

First, something pops up and causes the organization to launch what it considers its A#1 project. You are named the project lead, results are specified, plans are made and significant resources are dedicated to deliver success over the next four months. At first, things are humming along smoothly - you even pass your initial Jacks or Better peer review with flying colors.

Then, about the middle of month two, something happens and the organization decides to launch a new project that is now considered the new A#1. Rather than taking the time to: (1) finish what is already started (i.e. your project), or (2) officially halt your project in order to put "all hands on deck" for the new initiative, what happens is that a small drain of your project resources occurs. For example, one person is lost to the new project, or an edict comes down that everyone will spend some time each week on the new project. Now your project is second priority, the trigger that kicked off your project no longer feels as urgent, and the schedule starts to slip because you have lost resources.

As the project loses momentum and falls behind, sponsors and team members tend to lose their gusto and the project's resources become even more ripe for the picking. Soon, other projects (some of which may even be led by you) begin to steal away additional resources. Even if it only feels like a few days here and a few days there, it can lead to a death spiral. The slower a project moves, the easier a target it becomes for others to poach its resources. This is not a recipe for success.

Project Momentum - A Downward Spiral

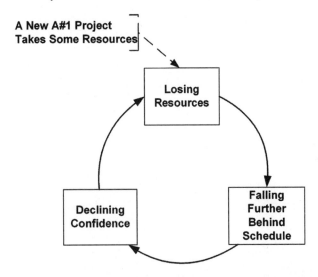

Eventually, the situation begins to resemble a quote from Bart Simpson when he is sent to the remedial class: "Let me get this straight. We're behind the rest of our class and we're going to catch up to them by going *slower*...that's cuckoo."

At some point, the lack of resources causes the project to become the wilted flower dying on the vine - one of many in the organization's garden. Even if these partially-alive projects are not draining a lot of time, they are still draining a non-trivial amount of people's attention and energy, causing stress because the goal is still valid, the responsibility still assigned, and the hope still there. Because the momentum has stopped but the project is not "over", there is lingering frustration and guilt.

While your organization may not want you to hear it, I want to tell you the cure for this situation:

**It is not only okay, but often required,
to cancel a project that has lost its momentum.**

49

If you don't believe me, trust Doyle Brunson:

For poker champions, there is nothing more important than knowing when you can't win.

As humans, it is difficult for us to fold things we have invested effort and resources in but which circumstances now dictate we must let go.

Stealing the Blinds

In poker, when in the first round of betting it appears no one else has a strong hand, opportunistic players will often try to bluff in order to quickly win the pot, a move known as "stealing the blinds." This strategy is a virtual necessity for winning in large tournaments.

If you decide to try to cash in by using this strategy and no one calls your bluff, then you will have successfully stolen the blinds. What separates the winners from the also-rans is how they decide to play after their bluff, when an opponent with a strong hand raises. If you are in this position, you have three main options:

One option is to re-raise and go all-in, showing that you cannot be pushed around. Typically, this all-in turns into an "all-out," when the truly strong hand quickly calls your bet and wins the pot.

A second option is to avoid the situation altogether by never attempting to steal the blinds. Unfortunately, this option requires giving up a proven winning strategy, thus, putting yourself at a serious disadvantage to the other, more aggressive players.

The third, and preferred, option is to realize that while you made what seemed like a good play at the time, the situation has now changed. As others bet, you learned more information; therefore, as much as it pains you to do so, you will have to cut your losses, fold the hand, and focus on a future one you can win.

There is no shame in getting caught trying to be aggressive and make a good play, only to realize you can't pull it off this time. Likewise, stepping up and folding stalled projects is not a sign of weakness nor ineffectiveness; in fact, it is just the opposite. What is weak and ineffective is forcing people to pretend as if the inactive projects are still continuing, thus allowing these projects to:

- Consume precious resources that could be used to strengthen other viable projects.
- Tarnish your image and degrade your credibility as a leader.
- Sap the morale of the project team members as they are forced to carry yet another thing around that drains their energy.

By taking the bolder, and in the long-term, more effective step of formally folding a project, you resolve the emotional and time drain on people, enabling them to focus on the projects where their efforts can most contribute to success. In addition, you reflect the realities of today's rapidly changing world: "While we thought this was the A#1 idea a few months ago, we are now focused on something more important." You also provide a natural trigger for those who set the organization's priorities to revisit: "Are we sure this new A#1 is actually more important than our last A#1?"

As Amarillo Slim once said:

Raise or fold – but never ever just call.

When project momentum stalls out, you must take action to put more resources into the pot, or else, fold the hand. What are you waiting for? The action is on you. Go find that withered project that has been stuck in your head throughout this section, and prune it.

BEATING THE ODDS

CHAPTER 5

Getting Your Head in the Game:
Ensuring a Sufficient Time Span

You will never find time for anything.
If you want time, you must make it.
- Charles Buxton

In today's environment, the demands on our time are greater than ever before. Why? To start, most organizations have been streamlined to the point that one person performs what used to be the jobs of multiple people. Plus, a push for self-reliance and cost reduction enabled by Microsoft Office, PCs, cell phones, Blackberrys, and other technology has led to a significant reduction in our administrative support. On top of all that, we work in a world of global competition, which means we can no longer simply perform our jobs; we must also take the time to improve and change what we are doing in order to stay competitive.

Against all this, how do we stay effective? One popular strategy is to become a master of multi-tasking. After all, if we have too much to do, shouldn't the answer be to do multiple things at once? This approach has become so prevalent in our society that I even spotted a "Queen Multi-Tasker" doll in a store recently. Unfortunately, the problem with this strategy is that for all but the simplest tasks, successful multi-tasking is a myth. Don't believe me? Try this test.

The Cell Phone Parking Test. This weekend, drive your car to a safe spot. Take out your cell phone and call someone you need to have an important conversation with. Once you get into the conversation, attempt to parallel park your car while maintaining the flow and content of your conversation. Regardless of whether you use a hands-free device, you will quickly realize that even these moderately simple tasks require too much focused mental attention to be done well simultaneously.

Sometimes it is hard to quantify and accept the inefficiencies and mistakes we make as we try to juggle multiple things at once. A situation that clarified this for me once and for all, and one that probably too many readers are familiar with, is trying to play online poker and do work at the same time. Trust me – you will lose! And I am not just talking about in the poker game. After all, if you try to complete two tasks at once and you clearly see your poker chips rapidly shrinking away in one window of your computer, how can you rationalize that the quality of your other work isn't similarly compromised?

More rigorous looks at the degradation of performance due to multi-tasking, recently featured on CNN and in *New York Times Magazine*[1], showed:

- Constant interruptions reduce productivity and leave people feeling tired and lethargic.
- The IQ of those who tried to juggle messages and work fell by 10 points.
- The drop in IQ was even more significant in men.
- Workers spent an average of only 11 minutes on a task before being interrupted.
- It took an average of 25 minutes for the worker to get back to the original task.

Peter Drucker scooped these reports, by a mere thirty-seven years, when in *The Effective Executive* he advocated the exact opposite of multi-tasking:

The only way to be effective is to consolidate large blocks of time. And the only way to consolidate blocks of time is to be able to say, "No!"

Making Things Happen

If you want to have a consistent, weekly poker game, here are three rules for making it happen:

1. **Make sure you block enough time.** A good rule of thumb is to block at least four hours. This allows people to get into the flow of the game and to let the cards even themselves out. Don't try to squeeze in an hour here and 90 minutes there - you will end up more frustrated than satisfied.
2. **Keep a consistent schedule,** e.g. every Tuesday 7:00 – 11:30. While on any given week it might be tempting to change the night – in the long run, having a dedicated schedule keeps the game alive.

---

[1] CNN.com, "Boost Your Brain Power at Work," 10/14/05 and *New York Times Magazine*, "Meet the Life Hackers," 10/16/05

3. **Show that you are committed.** Say "No!" to the things that come up in conflict. Can you go to the Braves game next Tuesday? No! Can you come to dinner with the McKendrick's? No! And so on.

While the above may sound harsh, this is what needs to happen if you want to have a dependable weekly game. Otherwise, what started out strong will quickly get pushed to the bottom of the pile.

Successful project leadership faces the same time challenges on at least two dimensions. The project leader needs:

1. Dedicated time to *plan* the project – as opposed to executing the plan.
2. Dedicated time to meet with key stakeholders to *promote* the effort. This includes understanding people's needs, providing status, and receiving input and feedback.

For project planning, the same three rules needed to create a successful weekly poker game apply:

1. **Make sure you block enough time.** It takes significant time to make the mental shift out of the day-to-day firefighting to get into a big picture planning mode. If enough time is not dedicated for planning, the *urgent* issues may get addressed but the *important* issues are continually put off until next time. Eventually, it is these important issues that come back to haunt you. Therefore, a good rule of thumb is to allow yourself at least a solid half day per week to get into the right mental state for planning, and ensure you work through all of the project issues, including both the urgent and the important. Don't try to squeeze in an hour here and 90 minutes there.
2. **Keep a consistent schedule**. If you want to greatly increase the odds that the project planning time will happen, don't simply think, "I will block at least four hours sometime each week." Instead, give this

planning a dedicated time on your schedule that all team members will know and can come to expect (and maybe even respect).

3. **Show that you are committed.** Just say, "No!" to the things that come up in conflict. Can you attend Judy's going away party? No! Can you sit in on a vendor presentation? No! After all, if these other activities are that important and you must attend, they are worth rescheduling around your planning time. Otherwise, once you start missing your sessions, planning will fall out of your routine and you will be back in constant fire-fighting mode.

Potentially even more dangerous than failing to dedicate time to do project planning is failure to dedicate adequate time to spend with people outside the project team on project promotion.

It can take a large group of people to make a project but just a small number to break a project. Making it more challenging, many of the project stakeholders that can most impact success or failure are not under any kind of formal control of the project leader. The following diagram shows many of the common classes of stakeholders that will impact the project's ability to reach its desired outcomes.

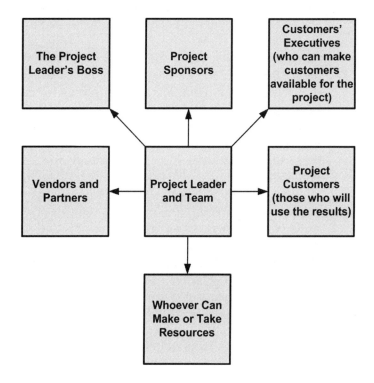

While projects often start with adequate plans to continually engage all of these stakeholder groups, once the projects get rolling and schedules get tight, project leaders are too easily tempted to cut time with stakeholders in favor of "working on the project." To combat this, stick to these three rules:

1. **Block enough time**. A primary goal of project promotion is for external stakeholders to feel that they are partners in the project. It takes time to connect and to understand their hopes and fears. Generic emails and 60-second pitches might be one piece of the puzzle. However, you need to spend enough time face-to-face so that your stakeholders take comfort in a personal connection and are able to give honest input and answers.

2. **Keep a consistent schedule**. Don't wait until you need something from your stakeholders to schedule a meeting with them. If you do, you will basically be showing up with your hand out, and they are not likely to be sympathetic. Instead, from the outset of the project, get into a periodic routine where you meet to check status and make adjustments based on their needs. Don't worry. If everything is going well and you cut the meeting 15 minutes short, they will be all the happier. When you do need something, because you've invested in building a partnership, you can tackle the problem together. Otherwise, you'll just be asking for yet another favor (which they never seem to forget you owe them).

3. **Show that you are committed.** If you start canceling because other things have come up, stakeholders will do the same. This can quickly dissolve the partnership and reduce support for the effort. Then you are back to only calling on them when you are needy, and they will sense your desperation.

Ramping Up and Ramping Down

The above strategy for consolidating, scheduling, and protecting time is rarely easy, not that much fun, and in no way exciting. But in the long run, it does prove more effective than running back and forth, like an acrobat trying to keep ten plates spinning simultaneously, doing a little of this here and a little of that there.

When you are not focused, you waste a great deal of time in the mental and physical ramp up and ramp down required each time you switch tasks. The following diagram compares the overall effort required to switch back and forth between three projects versus consolidating time and attention to knock them out one after another:

The Impact of Ramping Up and Ramping Down on Performance and Schedules

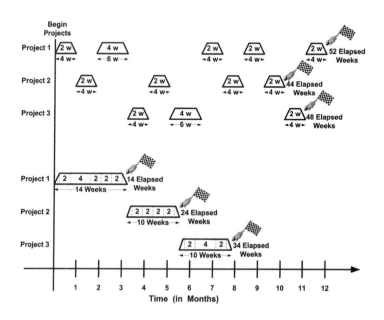

The four month difference in the overall schedule is due to the wasted time and energy of switching back and forth between efforts. As for multi-tasking, it has the same effect, except that now there are hundreds or thousands of interruptions and delays with micro-prep and micro-wrap. All that switching gears and running back and forth, no matter how "micro" we want to try to make it, still ends up burning a lot of time and energy and is a leading contributor to why we stay at work late, go home exhausted, and overrun our deadlines.

Poker and Projects Need Ample Time

One of the best things you can hear when you want to make money at a poker table is for one of the other players to say, "Let's hurry up and get started. I only have two hours until my girlfriend picks me up." Because successful poker playing requires patience, these players are at a serious disadvantage. They often play poorly because a premature deadline causes them to make bad decisions.

Some tournaments, like a noon no-limit tournament I recently played at the Luxor Casino in Las Vegas, are set up to move so fast that players don't feel they can play patiently. This tournament was set up to go from sixty players to one winner in two hours, which was extremely fast. What was the effect on the players? Many used the crazy deadline to excuse themselves from playing well. I could hear them saying things like, "There is nothing I can do," and "I'm just going to push all my chips in and hope for the best."

Project team members on artificial and too ambitious deadlines behave the same way. They try to force things when the timing is not right, or even worse, they begin to abdicate themselves of responsibility for doing a good job.

While it is certainly okay to have *aggressive* schedules, as project leaders we must ensure the schedules are <u>realistic</u> and <u>believable</u> by the team members. Team members who feel the goal is unrealistic may not do a quality job and/or may begin to put making themselves look good in front of project success. It is a big red flag if you start hearing, "There is nothing I can do," or "I did my part – the rest is up to someone else." Often, these indicate a need to adapt the plan to ensure the schedule is an honest one, given the specified results and the resources dedicated.

Leveraging Time: Bubble Management

Another great way to make money is to play in a poker game where people are trying to leverage their free time by playing cards and watching a big sporting event. After all, with commitments to work, family, friends, school, church, and everything else, doesn't it make sense for people to try to kill two birds with one stone - using what little free time they have to both play poker and watch sports?

61

Sure it does - just like it makes sense for you to use their divided attention to your advantage to take their money. Because your opponent is trying to do two things at once, they will probably do neither well. Not only will their poker decisions be worse than normal, they typically won't be able to truly get into and enjoy the sporting event. If you can focus solely on the poker, you should be able to take more money off your opponents than you would in a game with no distractions.

As project leaders, it is critical we enable our teams to be more like the focused player than the distracted player. One of my favorite terms for this is "bubble management." Bubble management means that you try to put the project team in a bubble to minimize the outside distractions that will compete for their attention. This includes minimizing a whole collection of interruptions from the large and complex to the small and routine:

Politics – Many projects take place in a volatile and changing political situation. As the project leader, it is your duty to shield your team from many of the political winds, so the team can focus on making progress.

Meetings – While there are some meetings for which team members are truly needed to provide input and ideas, project leaders should proactively ensure that the team is not overly bogged down in meetings, especially those meetings where the team could just as easily be brought up to speed afterward via email or a brief phone call.

Equipment – A team that is constantly distracted by dealing with laptops, cell phones, printers, networks, and other technology issues is not a team making rapid progress toward the project's goals. Part of setting up the bubble is ensuring the team has the tools needed to be successful.

Administrative and logistical tasks – Filling out timesheets, making copies, ordering lunch, booking travel, ordering supplies, and coordinating calendars all take time and attention. Keep delivery people focused on highest value activities by minimizing the need for administration and assigning remaining administrative tasks to staff who have the time and focus to complete this work.

Other – Anything else in your environment that is distracting, rather than enabling the team, needs to be minimized or eliminated by the bubble you provide.

Bubble management takes time to establish and effort to maintain. If you can strike the right balance, having enough of the big picture to ensure alignment with the overall direction, while eliminating the chaos and distractions that cause teams to slow down or even lock-up, you can greatly improve productivity and morale.

Can More Time Turn Into Too Much Time?

So far, we have examined scenarios where the time span for an effort is insufficient because:

- The deadline is ultra-aggressive to the point of not being credible.
- In trying to make things better by multi-tasking, the cost of switching gears actually makes matters worse.
- We fail to consolidate, schedule, and protect time to focus on the most crucial activities.

Nearly as dangerous for projects are the risks associated with too much time. *Beating the Odds* uses the term sufficient time span because sufficient indicates the right amount given the goals – neither too much nor too little. But why is too much time so dangerous?

Organizations, like people, have attention spans. And organizations, like people, have become more and more fragmented, constantly changing their focus and being distracted by interruptions. Therefore, it is critical to understand your environment by using the following test:

The Organizational Attention Span Test. To determine the length of your organization's attention span ask: How long does the typical A#1 project in your organization stay A#1 before something else comes along and bumps it to #2? That length of time is your organization's attention span. While it used to be measured in years, most organizations today seem to have an attention span of three months or less.

To have a sufficient time span for our projects, our time must be long enough to get the work done, but also short enough to be delivered within one attention span cycle (e.g. ~three months). But Wait! Aren't many of our projects too large and complex to be completed within the organization's attention span? So what do we do?

The key to maintaining a sufficient time span when in charge of a large project is to break it into increments. Each increment must be small enough to deliver *value* within the organizational attention span. Each time we deliver an increment that is seen as successful, the organization's attention span is refreshed and we are granted another three months to continue. Build success one increment at a time.

Getting Focused

There is no magic formula for getting focused and maximizing the use of your time, it simply requires a series of painful, hard choices.

The number-one thing that the average player can do to immediately improve his game is to quit calling pre-flop raises unless he also has a genuine raising hand.
Ken Warren, *Winner's Guide to Texas Hold'em Poker*

Likewise, in business the number one thing you can do to improve your success rates is quit doing things that aren't vitally important to your goals. Start by changing how you manage your to-do list. If you don't keep a list, start. Organize your to-do list from top to bottom by *importance*, not urgency. While you should highlight the urgent, always start from the top down in planning your day and picking your next activity.

Organize by Importance, not Urgency

#	*Do*	*Importance*	*Urgency*
1	Finish prototype	AAA	A
2	Hire new marketing person - Write job description	AA	C
3	Complete proposal for Minnesota	A	A
4	Respond to New York RFP	A	C
5	Meet with Peter	A	C
6	Attend conference in Boston	C	A
7	Follow up on assisting Todd	C	C
8	Finalize the 2006 Business Analyst Course Catalog	C	C
9	Follow up on exec. retreat RFP	C	C
10	Pick up suit at drycleaner	D	A

Writing things down and organizing by importance helps maintain the focus that is needed to stay out of fire fighting mode and ensure sufficient time for each activity.

Play Tight-Aggressive

Tight-aggressive is the style practiced by poker professionals the world over. It boils down to a single principle: focus all resources squarely on the most valuable opportunities. As project leaders, focus your time and attention by:

- Refusing to multi-task on difficult activities.
- Consolidating sufficient blocks of time.

- Keeping a consistent schedule for activities that repeat daily, weekly, monthly, or yearly.
- Showing you are committed by saying "No!" to the urgent tasks, and instead, give priority to the most important activities.
- Encouraging those around you to do the same.

Focusing your time and attention in this tight-aggressive style is just as strong a strategy on the job as it is in the cardroom.

Tight-aggressive players don't come to play,
they come to win.
- Alan Schoonmaker, Ph.D., *The Psychology of Poker*

CHAPTER 6

Short-stacks, Maniacs,
Dead-money, and Grinders:
Driving Project Success

Today's professional must demonstrate the
ability and inclination to tolerate
chaos, ambiguity, and lack of knowledge,
and to function effectively in spite of them.
- Karl Burton, systems designer for Xantel

Driving Project Success

Functioning effectively in poker, in business, and in life requires the ability to navigate the chaos, ambiguity and incomplete information that make up the environment of our world. Chapters 1 through 5 provided a roadmap for succeeding in this world.

To recap:

- Most projects fail to deliver the desired business results.
- Most poker players fail to win money over the long run.
- The key to success is not found in advanced topics with seductive names.
- Success comes from the discipline to consistently apply fundamentals.
- The four fundamentals for setting up a game you can win are:
    1. Understanding your specified business results.
    2. Having an adaptable plan.
    3. Dedicating resources.
    4. Ensuring a sufficient time span for success.

Sound simple enough? Sure. Do most of us feel like we are doing this today? Sure. The problem is that too often we only "kinda" have these pieces fully in place.

Taking the time to fully establish the four elements for success will <u>not</u> eliminate the chaos, ambiguity, and lack of knowledge from your world. Rather, putting all four of these elements in place creates a stable platform for moving the project forward across rough terrain. It is helpful to think of these four elements as the wheels on a car, allowing the project to move forward, accelerate, stop, and make turns to avoid obstacles. Progress occurs in a relatively balanced and controlled manner as the project leader drives the effort toward the goal.

When projects have less than all four "wheels" fully inflated, some combination of stability, safety, and speed is sacrificed as the effort zooms along on only three, two, or even one wheel. Common unstable project configurations are given below (with additional detail in Appendix C):

Unicycles – Under close and honest examination, many of the most unbalanced and slowest moving projects have only one of the four elemental wheels. These efforts often mimic the herky-jerky forward and backward progress of a juggler on a unicycle. While an expert rider can sometimes make progress on a unicycle, more often than not the whole thing comes quickly crashing down.

At the poker table, if you have only one of the four elements, they probably have a nickname for you; and, if you are a "fish," having lots of money but little else, they definitely have a seat for you.

Two-wheelers – By adding a second element to the project foundation, you develop the potential for making substantial progress. However, when driving a motorcycle it is advisable to wear a helmet because they have a tendency to be unstable and vulnerable to changes in the terrain and the environment.

Many poker players fall into the two wheel category. Find someone with only money and time, and you have hooked a "live one." Spot an open seat next to someone with money and results, but blindly following a process they can't adapt, and you can take money off that "A–B–C player."

Three-wheelers – To the casual observer, three wheeled cars seem capable of doing most of the things a four wheeled car can do. However, three-wheelers are more likely to tip at high speeds, run off the road on challenging corners, and take longer to deliver you safely to your destination. Three wheeled projects mimic the behavior of their automotive counterparts.

In poker, having three of the four elements in place is a lot like having the second best hand. While the best hand is a winner and nothing hands are easily thrown away, it is having the second best hand that is truly dangerous. Having something that is <u>almost</u> a winner causes players in poker and projects to invest a great deal of resources and emotion, only to lose out in the end.

Poker players that are "close but no cigar," lacking one of the four elements, are everywhere and go by the following names:

Name	Missing Element
Short-stacks	Dedicated resources
Maniacs	Specified results
Dead-money	Adaptable plans
Grinders	Sufficient time span

Short-stacks

Short-stacks are players who are focused on results, have adaptable plans, and have the sufficient time needed to reach their goals. The problem is their chip stack. Through some series of circumstances, they are now at the point where they have few chips left, and therefore, lack the dedicated resources required to make significant progress. Most of the time short-stacks are on a path to being knocked out of the game. The only question is whether it will be a quick implosion or a slow, painful death.

How can short-stacks get back into a position for success? Some poker games allow players to "re-buy," putting up more cash to get more chips. Whether or not re-buying is advisable depends on the situation.

- **Do not re-buy if even with the new resources you still won't reach a critical mass for success.**
  Suppose everyone started a tournament with $1,000 in chips. You are down to $500 while the leaders have over $5,000. Does it really make sense to go to the ATM to buy another $1,000 in chips only to still be outnumbered greater than three to one? (Answer: Not if your goal is winning money.)
- **Do not re-buy if you became a short-stack because you are in over your head.** Often players are a short-stack for a simple reason: they are being out-played. Their opponents might be better players, or for some reason the short-stack is off her game that day. If this is the situation, re-buying is probably little more than throwing your money away.

- **Do re-buy if the additional resources will complete your foundation for success.** If you are certain you are focused on results, following an adaptable plan (one that is better than your opponent's), and have sufficient time to not only recoup your losses but also to come out on top – then by all means re-buy.

If you are a short-stack on a project, having everything but ample, dedicated resources, the question of whether to re-buy (making a renewed investment in project resources) is similar.

- **Do not re-buy if even with the new resources you still won't reach a critical mass for success.** Suppose you are leading an effort that would take five people and $250,000 to deliver, but all you have is one person and $50,000. If there is an opportunity to add a second person and another $50,000, but nothing beyond, what do you do? You do not re-buy because doing so would only set your project up for an even bigger loss.
- **Do not re-buy if you became a short-stack because you are in over your head.** If you don't speak up every once in a while to say, "I'm in too deep," either you aren't venturing far enough into the deep end, or when your efforts do get into trouble, you aren't speaking up soon enough. Many executives want their leaders to venture out to take on large challenges. They understand, and even respect, the occasional call for help, and will often work to help get you the resources required.
- **Do re-buy if the additional resources will complete your foundation for success.** Sometimes one bad beat or bad break has caused resource problems with an otherwise solid project. If this is the case, make every effort to get additional resources.

71

What about situations where there is no effective way to re-buy? Sometimes the rules of the situation mean you can't just buy the additional resources you need (e.g. when you need more of your external customers' time, or when you have entered a poker tournament with no re-buys).

When strong tournament poker players get short-stacked, they know to switch from their normal playing style to a final stand mode. In this mode, you want to:

- Be patient.
- Pick your spots carefully.
- Make your stand by putting all your chips into the pot on that hand.

Most of the time, because the short-stack bets all of their chips, everyone else folds and they win the pot. This increases the resources available for their next big stand. When they do get called, they have a good chance of doubling up, having waited for the right opportunity.

When short-stacked on projects, the same three principles apply. Be patient, pick an opening, and seize the opportunity by bringing all resources to bear. If you realize you don't have adequate resources to deliver the entire project, look for an increment that you can carve off and conquer. Forget trying to make progress across the entire effort; instead pick a piece that is realistic, and that once delivered, people will say:

1. Wow! We are actually making tangible progress.
2. This is already making a significant impact on the business.

Because so much of what happens in organizations' day-to-day activities doesn't seem to make progress, nor make a strong impact, the successful delivery of even a small increment will often help your project stand out from the crowd. Once people see and feel this progress, leverage the opening to make your case: "If we could add additional resources, here is how we could accelerate progress and deliver an even larger impact."

Poker Sidebar: Short-stacked in Tournament Play

In most tournament play, poker chips are finite resources, meaning you can't put in more money once your chips are gone. If you find yourself staring down at a short-stack with your tournament life on the line, here are a few ways to get back on top.

1. **Concentrate your attack.** When you are short-stacked, just calling bets is no longer an option. Instead, you should decide at the beginning of the hand if it is worth all of your chips or not. If it is, use your chips in a concentrated attack. On a monster hand (A-A, K-K, A-K) attack with approximately a third of your chips pre-flop, followed by an all-in on the flop. This will allow you to both juice the pot pre-flop and eliminate your competition after the flop. If your hand is strong but not a monster (A-J, A-10, or any pair), you should attack immediately by going all-in pre-flop. This play represents a very strong hand to your competitors, driving out callers.

2. **Play your position.** Maximizing your betting position is an important aspect of tournament play, and it becomes critical as your stack gets shorter. When short-stacked, you want to play in hands with as little competition as possible. So wait for hands where you are close to the dealer button and no one has called in front of you. Combining this tactic with a concentrated attack will give you the best chance for taking down the pot. Always remember, if you aren't the first bettor in a hand, then you are joining a pot with automatic competition and jeopardizing your tournament life.

3. **Know when to shift gears.** Change into short-stacked mode too soon and you will sacrifice a chance to be dealt a monster. Engage too late and people will not be afraid to call your puny all-ins. Your short-stacked approach should kick in when your stack falls roughly below ten times the big blind.

Maniacs

Like short-stacks, maniacs are poker players with only three of the four basic elements. They have resources ($$$), time, and adaptable plans but they are missing specified *business* results. Instead of being driven by creating financial value, they are driven by something else. It might be a need to blow off steam, get their aggression out, show off, or escape. Whatever drives them, it is definitely <u>not</u> a focus on making money. Maniacs often raise, and re-raise with virtually no concern for the quality of their cards, the position they are in, or their opponents' chip stacks. A maniac might be a habitually bad player, or a strong player who has temporarily gone on-tilt and is "throwing a party," putting money into virtually every pot.

Recalling the lessons of Chapter 2, there may be nothing wrong with playing like a maniac (i.e., it is okay to chase fun and excitement rather than dollars at the poker table if it is *your* money and these results are valuable to *you*). However, on projects at work, you simply cannot allow yourself to fall into the trap of being driven by anything other than the specified business results. You are being paid to deliver results that will contribute to an eventual positive return for the enterprise.

How can maniacs get refocused on their desired results? If you are playing poker like a maniac and know you want to get back to focusing on money:

- Step away from the table, walk over to the bar (or kitchen) and pull out a cocktail napkin.
- Take a second to breathe, think, and decide: For the next few hours I am playing poker with _____'s money in order to _____.
- Write it down, fold it up, and put it in your wallet where you won't lose it.
- Remind yourself throughout the rest of the night that you are going to pull your note out when you get home to judge your success.

On projects, if you are leading like a maniac, focusing on fun, chasing the perception of success rather than the real thing, or being seduced by the sizzle of technology or other exciting solutions:

- Step away from the day-to-day firefighting.
- Meet with the sponsor or someone who can adequately represent those bankrolling the effort.
- Review the specified results document used to launch the project.

Napkin Specified End Results Template

Project Name: _____

Desired Results – The Ends We Are After:
(In terms of outcomes and expressed with the project currency)

_____

_____

Who is Bankrolling the Effort:_____

Are They All-In?   ( ) Yes   ( ) No

If you and your sponsor are still in agreement that the intentions are valid, take two additional steps:

1. Ask yourself if, as the project leader, you can focus on using these results to drive your decisions and actions. If you can't, perhaps the best course of action is to find someone else who can.
2. If you can commit to the results, go ahead and make yourself a napkin version to carry around in your wallet as a personal beacon and to have available whenever you need to keep your team members from chasing different goals.

While it might seem that the idea of putting your project vision on a napkin and carrying it around is meant to be humorous, in fact it is a serious, literal suggestion. Everyone is so overwhelmed by information crammed in three-ring binders or hidden away on a laptop, that it is easy to lose the forest for the trees.

One consultant I work with, Ed Wynn, has found a technique even more effective than the napkin. Whenever we fly out to work on a new project, as soon as the fasten seat belt sign goes off, Ed says: "Put the notebooks, documents, and computers away. If we can't concisely describe the project from what's in our head, then we don't really have a handle on what's going on." He then reaches forward and pulls out the air sickness bag, flips it over, and asks, "Now tell me again – what are the expected business results of this effort?" Every time we have gone through this exercise, it has greatly helped us get re-focused on the core goals of the effort and quickly identify what aspects are crystal clear versus what issues remain murky. When we arrive at the client site, we repeat the exercise with them, asking them to speak off the top of their heads about the project goals and summarize them on one page. This test quickly illuminates if they are solution focused, describing the outputs, or business driven, focusing on outcomes.

Dead-money

Dead-money is poker slang for players who have the time and money to reach their goals, but without an adaptable game plan strong enough to win the game. They are in over their heads, lacking the experience and expertise needed for a reliable shot at success. It should be noted that just because someone is dead-money in a particular poker game does not mean they are not smart, hardworking, capable, or even brilliant in other areas of their lives. After all, just because someone is a great lawyer, does not make them a great poker player, any more than it makes them a great plumber or great opera singer.

Why are project leaders so often dead-money on their projects? Frequently, it is because they were promoted to leadership positions because they were great "doers" but these skill-sets did not necessarily translate to being great leaders. The organization has not invested in them, and they have not invested in themselves to develop the necessary leadership skills, including understanding people, dealing with politics, and motivating teams. When their projects get into trouble, they don't manage their way out by leveraging other people, but rather try to lock themselves in a room and do it all themselves.

What to do when you feel like dead-money? If you find yourself feeling like dead-money week after week:

1. **Recognize you might not have an underlying process to plan around.**
   - If you have never played a lot of poker or studied a lot about it, why would you expect to be anything but dead-money? Where would a process for winning come from? Watching poker on TV? You watch a lot of football on TV; think you're ready for the NFL? Besides, when they edit tournaments down to one or two hours for television, they cut out the boring stuff – and *it is the boring stuff that wins tournaments.*
   - If you have been more of an individual contributor than a leader of others in your career, you may not have developed a process for leading people. Being smart and hardworking are not the same as being experienced in a particular area. Just as you shouldn't get frustrated the first time you try to make sushi, give a public speech, or try to hula-hoop, you shouldn't get down on yourself for not having a leadership process. Ready yourself by investing in a repeatable leadership approach.

2. **Develop your process.** If lack of process is an issue, there are at least three ways to improve your game plan:

- **Figure it out on the fly.** Playing to learn is great for supplementing your knowledge, but it is a difficult, risky, and expensive approach that your sponsors may not want to finance. Instead, take on smaller projects and tables first. Focus on specific elements with which you are comfortable and get help with those you aren't.
- **Leverage credible sources.** There are a lot of excellent books on how to improve your game that walk you through processes for winning. Read two or three and extract a process that works for you. You will quickly recoup the investment and more.
- **Learn from others.** Find someone more experienced than yourself to be your mentor. Get them to teach you their process. You will be surprised that even in competitive poker and business environments, people often can't help but open up and share their secrets if you show true interest in learning from them.
  - You can see the impact of mentoring in professional poker where many of the up-and-comers acknowledge the guidance of experienced veterans. Among the most well known pairings are Men "The Master" Nguyen with his cousin, David "The Dragon" Pham and 2004 World Series of Poker runner-up, David Williams, who credited European star, Marcel Luske, for helping him reach his full potential.
  - While many business executives may seem too busy to want to take the time to teach, this image is an illusion. Virtually every leader I've met desires spending time with those who truly want to learn. It helps the company by developing people, helps those being coached to succeed, and helps the executives fulfill their desire to share what they know and make a difference in people's lives.

3. **Consider changing games.** If you don't have the desire to develop a process for winning or you feel the cost of learning will be too great – change games.
   - Maybe poker isn't what you need. Maybe you should be playing blackjack, hearts, war, or something you have already mastered.
   - Perhaps becoming a leader isn't your calling, and instead, you should become an expert in a skill that focuses on individual contribution. Or, maybe leadership is right for you but you need to lead a different type of effort. The bottom line is that being a leader without a leadership process is unsustainable. You either need to raise your game or fold and move on.

Grinders

Grinders are players who take a very conservative, long-term approach to winning at poker. They have a focus on winning money, adaptable plans, and financial resources. The problem with grinders, if it should even be called a problem, is that they have too long of a time span. Compared to short-stacks, maniacs, and dead-money players, grinders are much more frustrating and much less profitable to play with (those tight bastards).

While grinding it out, waiting for nothing but the best hands and never risking too much, can be a successful strategy for long-term profitability in poker, it does not always transition well to the business world. Grinding requires focus, patience and an extreme willingness to sacrifice fun and excitement for eventual financial rewards. In poker, if the grinder can remain true to their strategy, it can work out well since others around them are not willing to overcome their natural tendencies to want fun and excitement.

When leading projects on the other hand, success requires working *with* rather than *against* the natural tendencies of those around you. Because most of the stakeholders will not be infinitely patient, a textbook grind it out approach of "take all necessary time to get it right" is almost never practical. In today's world, projects need momentum for survival and to break through the resistance and obstacles that spring up along the way. Engineers define momentum as the product of mass times velocity. If your project is moving at a slow velocity, and therefore with low momentum, it is:

- Susceptible to being stopped or knocked backward by even the slightest impediment.
- At risk of not delivering within the organizational attention span, and thus, at risk of dying on the vine.

Successful project leaders set up their teams, schedules, and attitudes to be more urgent than business as usual. They follow the advice of Matt Damon's character in *Rounders*:

> *I learned how to win a little bit at a time, but finally I learned this: If you're too careful, your whole life can become a <bleep>ing grind.*

Avoid the Second Best Hand

Remember, having something that is almost a winner is the most dangerous position in poker and on projects. Ensure that you have all four elements fully inflated in terms of results, plans, resources, and time. Not one, not two, not three, not kinda all four, but firmly all four. Having your vehicle ready doesn't put you at the finish line or even at the final table, but it does get you in the game.

PART 2

People Are People

If you know poker, you know people;
and if you know people, you got the whole
dang world lined up in your sights.
– Mel Gibson in *Maverick*

BEATING THE ODDS

CHAPTER 7

Poker Is a Game of People:
Is Project Leadership Any Different?

*No matter how much you may want to think of
poker as a card game played by people...
think of it as a game about people that happens
to be played with cards.*
- Phil Hellmuth, 1989 World Series of Poker champion

Want to find out where the vast majority of poker players focus their attention? It's simple; just ask them how their last poker game went. Most likely, they will tell you one of two things:
1. It was great - I had great *cards*.
2. It was terrible - I had terrible *cards*.

Want to know where the vast majority of project leaders focus their attention? Ask them to give you a status of how their project is going. Most often they answer one of two ways:
1. Great - we are on *schedule* and on *budget*.
2. It's okay - we are a little behind our *schedule* and *budget*.

While cards, schedules, and budgets certainly are important, they are not where the strongest performers focus their attention. Poker legend Doyle Brunson says it best:

Poker is a game of people. If you remember that, you can bounce your opponents around like tumbleweeds in Texas. If you forget, Lord have mercy on your bankroll!

Is leadership any different? Not according to one eye-catching book title:

Work Would Be Great If It Weren't for the People
- Ronna Lichtenberg

If you find this title's sentiment appealing, the main problem with this wishful thinking is that it ain't gonna happen. The primary reason project leadership is such a demanding, and often rewarding, position is that most of the time you are being paid to *create value* with the *people you are given*. Even if somehow you could hire an entirely new "perfect" project team, it would not eliminate your people problem. You would still have human customers, sponsors, bosses, and peers. You can't replace them with computers, cyborgs, clones, or collies.

So, what do you do? The first key to managing people is to understand the difference between mandating and influencing. To illustrate, the following example is from a memorable showdown I had with one of the strongest regulars in my weekly poker game. As the hand started, I was distracted while acting as host for the night and accidentally revealed that my best card was a 5. We placed our initial bets, and the flop came:

Me   **My Opponent**

My opponent, a strong conservative player, bet his standard medium-large bet. On any other day, I would have folded since all I had was a pair of 5's, particularly with two monster cards like ace and king showing on the board. Yet, for some unknown reason, I decided to call his bet.

The next card came: the queen of spades.

Me   **My Opponent**

I studied the board to identify all the cards my opponent could have that would put him in the lead. I knew I was behind and he knew I was behind; so, he decided to *make* me fold with a big bet. As stressed earlier, if you are playing primarily to win money and you know it is a bad financial bet, you *must* fold. Yet, for some crazy reason I just knew I was going to have a Hollywood ending with a 5 coming on the river to give me three 5's to win the pot. So instead of folding, I called his bet and pushed in a stack of chips. When the river card was flipped, did I get my 5? Of course not. It was the 10 of spades.

Me   **My Opponent**

My opponent had me beat if he had an A, K, Q, J, 10 or any two spades. He went all-in, pushing in a huge bet dwarfing the substantial sum already in the pot. He knew this would make me fold, since to call and lose would finish me for the night.

What did I do? I did something I probably would only do once or twice a year. I called him. He shrieked amazed and disgusted, "How can you call that?! There is no way that you can call that with a pair of 5's!!!" Unfortunately for him, he was on a bluff, flipping over a pair of 3's and losing the hand.

's <u>not</u> that sometimes you get
on a bad play. The point is
er table. No matter how
your reasoning is:

**people do something
on't want to do.**

estimate the ability of poker players to
ad what to do. No matter how unreasonable
as simply not going to fold that hand. My oppo-
early and consistently communicated a straightfor-
d, logical, and compelling case as to what course of
action I should take. Yet, I chose the opposite.

Is project leadership any different? Can you make people
do things they don't want to do? Or, can you only influence?

The favored answer to this question has shifted dramatically in the last decade. Prior to the information age
and the employee shortages of the late 90's, the responses
to this question were split. Some said: "it's my way or the
highway," others: "influence." Now, more and more, I
hear: "I know I can't make them do what I say; so, I guess
I can only influence."

Unfortunately, a high percentage of those who say, "I
can only influence," haven't successfully translated that
philosophy into effective action. They either continue to
rely on intimidation and big sticks, or they do nothing and
accept a free-for-all. Their quandary reminds me of par-
ents who have decided that spanking is not a proper way
to discipline but have not developed alternative motivational techniques, and are at a loss as to how to effectively
influence their children's behavior.

How do you do better? The first step is to look at your
situation on the job and decide if your environment is one
in which your key team members are professionals who:

- Exercise self-direction and initiative.
- Want to be empowered.
- Resist being micro-managed.
- Resent being yelled at and treated like children.

87

If these are true, you should accept that cra[
whip is futile in your world. You must learn to eff[
use influence as your primary tool to motivate and[
Otherwise, you risk your team calling your bluff a[
most inopportune moment.

In her book, *Radical Careering,* Sally Hogshead lays o[
her team's research as to what motivates the 65 millio[
Gen X workers born between 1960 and 1980:

- 95% prefer working autonomously to being managed.
- They answer the question - Which is your idea of
  professional hell? - in the following ways:
    - 75% - Disrespectful boss or coworkers.
    - 16% - Being micro-managed.
    - 5% - Low pay.
    - 4% - Long hours.

Up until a few years ago, it was tempting to dismiss this
generation and their desire for empowered autonomy as
inconsequential to your success. Now, these attitudes are on
the verge of reaching a tipping point to become the norm,
not the exception. Because Gen X workers currently represent over one-third of the workforce, their entrepreneurial
mind-set, and inclination to respect ability over authority,
can no longer be ignored. Therefore, leaders must adapt and
learn to effectively manage and leverage this generation if
they are to continue to succeed as leaders in the future.

Influencing People

While most of us like the idea of being able to successfully influence others (as evidenced by Dale Carnegie selling
over 15 million copies of *How to Win Friends and Influence
People*), the notion of having to apply a touchy-feely skill for
making it happen repels many. If you are one of these people,
you can relax. *Beating the Odds* lays out a common sense,
problem-solving based approach for influencing people. This
approach, commonly known as stakeholder analysis, is presented as a four step technique that can be practiced at the
poker table and applied on the job.

- **Step 1 – Motivation.** The first step is admitting: "I have a problem and need to change my behavior."
- **Step 2 – Discovery.** Take the time to identify your stakeholders - not just the people paying for the project but anyone who can impact your success or can be impacted by your success. While there is benefit to be gained by analyzing any and all stakeholders, practicality dictates we prioritize the list to document and focus on the primary stakeholders – those who can have the largest impacts. These are the people you most need to influence.
- **Step 3 – Assessment.** Once you have identified your primary stakeholders, seek to understand what each individual is after in regard to the effort. What are *their* desired ends? In other words, if the project is successful, what do they stand to gain? Knowing this gives you an idea of what will influence them.
- **Step 4 – Specification.** Look for the overlap between each individual's desired result and the behaviors you need for success. Focus their time and energy on the activities and decisions that are win-win to both the project and that individual.

How to Practice Stakeholder Analysis at the Poker Table

Before your next poker game, first ask yourself: "Do I need to influence the decisions of those around me to meet my goals?" If you are not playing primarily to win money, then it probably doesn't matter. However, if your goal is to win money, start by making a list of those players who you expect to win the most from, or are most at risk of losing to. Then, describe what you believe their priorities are in terms of desired end results for the game. If it is your weekly home game of regulars, you can easily create this list beforehand. Even if you are out playing strangers in a large poker room, go ahead and grab a pen and a cocktail napkin. Usually, you can figure out pretty quickly if someone is there to make a living or if they are just there to blow off steam, drink beer, and throw their money around - *"c'mon let's gamble!"* A quick napkin analysis might look like:

Player	Suspected End Result
Chris	Socializing
Cowboy Guy	Gambling
Dana	Drinking
K.K.	Proving her aggressiveness
Wes	Winning money

The key to influencing people is to recognize that if you can give them what <u>they</u> are after, then they will give you what <u>you</u> are after - in this case, their money. Based on each individual's suspected end results, you can develop potential strategies for making the situation mutually beneficial.

Sample Stakeholder Analysis at the Poker Table

Your desired end results: ___Win Money___

Player and Desired End Result	Strategies to Help Them Meet **Their** Needs	Strategies to Help Them Meet **Your** Needs
Chris Socializing	Give him the stories he is looking for so he comes back to deposit money week after week.	Play solid and make sure you are the one taking his entertainment allowance.
Cowboy Guy Gambling	Feed his gambling rush by playing loose on small hands, keeping the game fast-paced and dramatic.	When you have a good hand, push the action. When you don't, fold. Remember, never try to bluff a gambler.
Dana Drinking	Keep the fridge stocked.	Make sure you are winning more than you spend on beer.
K.K. Proving her aggressive-ness	Stoke her wild play by showing your cards when she bluffs you out of a good hand, challenging her plays, betting big, etc.	When you have a good hand, check to her, re-raise over the top, and dare her to call.
Wes Winning money	Keep your game stocked with players who freely part with their cash.	Take money from the others. Only challenge him when you have a monster hand.

Taking the time to analyze people's motives can immediately and dramatically impact the size of your bankroll, especially if you can keep focused on people while others focus on the cards and the excitement. Always remember to consider who else is in the hand and what their end game is before you decide whether or not to bet, raise, or fold.

Stakeholder Analysis on the Job

As a project leader, you need to understand not only the project's end results but also the desired end results of each of your team members. Unlike in poker, where the goals of the other players are often in direct conflict with yours, on projects there is often a large overlap between each individual's desired end results, your desired end results, and those of the project.

Overlapping Goals

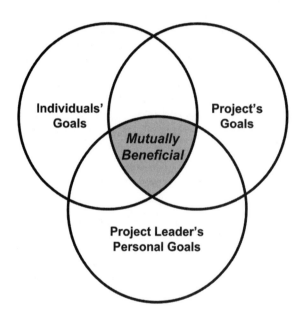

For example, consider a project where the desired end result is to <u>increase sales leads</u> through an improved website and marketing campaign. Looking at the stakeholders and their individual goals, you can develop potential strategies for making the situation mutually beneficial.

Sample Project Stakeholder Analysis

Project end results: Increase sales leads _____

Stakeholder (and Role)	Individual Goal	"Win-win" Motivational Strategy
Annie (Director of Sales)	More sales to increase her commission.	Continuously promote that her time and input are necessary because: "If we do this well, it will generate more, qualified leads."
George (Team Member)	Chance to learn new things.	Provide the opportunity to use a new set of tools for building the website.
David (Team Member)	Exposure to executives.	Allow him to present monthly status reports to the executive round table.
Christina (Team Member)	Chance to travel.	Allow her to do the discovery needed with your European customers.
Mary (Project Sponsor)	Show that she's an innovator.	Where appropriate, choose leading edge technology, and help her promote to her boss that this project is ground breaking.

I am not suggesting that you should grossly redirect the project to focus solely on individuals' needs. Rather, by playing your cards correctly, you can leverage the abundant overlap between each individual's needs and the project's needs. This results in higher output from your team, yourself, and the overall project.

While this may seem like a common sense approach, it is radically different from what managers typically do. Most managers know what *they* want and don't take the time to analyze anyone else's motivation. Even when they *do* know what others need, because many of the choices would force them to put their own egos aside and force their personal needs to take a back seat, they fail to act. After all, it's not easy to pass up an opportunity that is personally appealing, and instead allow others to present to the executives and travel to Europe.

Separate yourself from management as usual by not only taking the time to care about what others desire but also by following through and putting their needs in front of yours. Your team will respect you for it and work all the harder to make the project a success.

To recap the fundamentals of stakeholder analysis:

1. Accept that in many situations, influencing is more effective than mandating.
2. Position those around you to reach their desired results, and they will assist you in reaching yours.
3. Take the time to:
   - Identify your stakeholders.
   - Discover their individual needs.
   - Assess the fit of their needs with the project's needs.
   - Specify strategies to *simultaneously* meet both project and individual needs.

Stakeholder Analysis – Part II

Once the merits and basics of stakeholder analysis are understood, the next question is often: "This sounds great on paper, but how can I identify these needs when dealing with real people?" Don't worry, it is actually far easier than most imagine. Virtually all people have a set of fundamental needs that should be explored. You can readily identify these needs since:

1. People drop clues unintentionally.
2. People drop clues intentionally.
3. You can ask them!

Poker Sidebar: Reading Tells

Because poker is more a game of people than a game of cards, developing the skill to read your opponents can quickly ratchet your game up to the next level. Almost every poker player has tells - physical clues or hints by which a player unknowingly reveals the strength of his hand. At the table, watch for the following three basic types of tells:

1. **Watch their face.** The poker players on T.V. aren't just trying to look cool by wearing sunglasses and pulled down hats; they are purposefully hiding their faces. Unconscious and uncontrollable physical tells may show on a player, so look for any facial tics or other signs of emotion. A slight frown may reveal a missed draw, while a twitch of a grin or widened eyes can signal trouble, so you had better run.

2. **Examine their timing.** Players often can't stop themselves from staring at their hand when dealt a big pair. A good way to read your opponents is to watch as they peek at their hole cards - the longer they stare, the bigger the pair.

3. **Observe their chip stacking.** Walk into any poker room these days, and you will see a wannabe Phil Ivey or Chris Ferguson, flaunting fancy chip tricks in hope of impressing or intimidating their opponents. Yet chip stacking can reveal as well as intimidate, so watch an opponent's chip handling closely to see if patterns emerge. Once you have their pattern down, watch for inconsistencies. Many players will stack differently before raising with a big hand, while others will slop their chips when they're nervous over a bluff.

If you think that these tells aren't that important, just ask 2003 World Series of Poker champ, Chris Moneymaker. He recognized that when his final opponent, Sammy Farha, shuffled his chips with his left hand, he was folding, and when he shuffled with the right, he was going to call. Cracking Farha's tell was a key to Moneymaker's miracle story, World Series bracelet, and $2.5 million prize purse.

If you take the time to actually focus on people, you may be surprised by how easy they are to read. At work, watch people's body language to see what makes them sit up, take notice, and give their undivided attention. Actively listen to them; what are their favorite buzzwords? What won't they stop talking about? When they talk about their job to others, what do they say? Even easier than all that - you can ask them. Periodically, sit down with team members, sponsors, customers, and others to ask, "What do you want to get out of this project? How are you going to judge your personal success? What experiences are you looking for?"

Discovering What Motivates People

Many frameworks exist for categorizing the fundamental needs of humans. One of the most widely known, and most highly borrowed and iterated, is Maslow's Hierarchy of Needs. I've found that a simplified version of this hierarchy, practically applied, works for both poker and projects. A common interpretation of this theory asserts that until more basic levels of needs are met, humans do not and cannot care about the higher levels. As an extreme example, if you are on an airplane when it becomes depressurized and the oxygen masks appear, at that precise moment there is no way you will care if you are hungry or tired or dislike the movie. The only thing you will focus on is getting oxygen to breathe. While five seconds earlier it might have seemed like the drink cart was the most important thing in the world, as soon as a lower level need, in this case air, is not being met, virtually all attention turns to satisfying that need.

Following is an illustration and brief summary of Maslow's needs hierarchy.

Maslow's Hierarchy of Needs

1. **Sustenance** – Physiological needs for survival, including air, shelter, food, and warmth.
2. **Safety** – Security needs, including protection from injury or attack.
3. **Community** – Social needs, including being accepted into a group and sharing common experiences.
4. **Esteem** – Admiration needs, including recognition for contribution and achievement.
5. **Self-actualization** – Fulfillment needs, including the desire to grow, develop, reach one's full potential, and make a meaningful contribution.

Sustenance

When people struggle for food and shelter they cannot focus well on anything else. If you are playing poker against someone whose primary goal truly is to put food on their table, my advice is to walk away from that game. They are most likely a combination of too desperate, too dangerous, or too good to meet your needs.

At work, while certainly it is true that earning a pay-check is a key reason many team members show up each day, most often their need to put food on the table is sufficiently met to the point where they focus further up the pyramid. The need for sustenance is not directly driving their daily decisions and actions.

This, however, is not always the case. When you have a team member or members whose compensation is not allowing them to put food on the table (literally) or to meet what they feel is the bare minimum required for their family obligations, you must take action. Either fight to secure them the compensation they need so they can turn their attention to the project's goals, or get them off the team so they are not distracting the project. Otherwise, you are at risk of having a net loss as they take more time, energy, and attention than they give back. If neither of these solutions is possible, as a last resort, relegate them to periphery roles where they are not on the critical path and thus, less likely to jeopardize the project. It is no more practical to expect someone whose sustenance needs are not being met to perform at high levels than it is to expect someone to finish writing an email on the plane before they put that oxygen mask over their nose and mouth.

Safety

Never use threats of violence to try to win at poker – it is morally wrong, period.

It is also a mistake to use the threat of losing one's job to motivate your team members. Not because it is immoral (it may or may not be), but because it is typically ineffective and counterproductive. Threatening people's jobs is detrimental because:

1. **Fear of losing one's job inhibits performance.**
   Many people freeze under pressure. They lose
   their creativity, candor, and courageousness.
   Resentment builds, and they tend to focus on
   covering their butt rather than reaching the project
   goals. The result is performance just high enough
   not to get fired, a target probably far below their
   maximum capability and often below what is
   needed for project success.
2. **You risk losing your best people.** When people
   feel threatened, their flight instinct kicks in and
   they will readily take their skills elsewhere. Once
   you lose a star performer, it becomes harder to get
   talented, new people. Word gets around if you are
   the type of leader that runs the best people off and
   may even set off a chain reaction, causing other
   valued team members to leave.
3. **The best you can get is compliance.** Ask yourself
   how you would respond, or how you have
   responded, when your job was threatened. Being
   onboard and motivated is not an all or nothing
   proposition; instead, varying levels exist, some
   much more beneficial than others. If you threaten a
   person's job, the most support you can expect to
   receive is compliance. Cooperation, commitment
   and partnership are what you want from project
   team members, not compliance.

Following is the full continuum of support people can
feel toward a project, depending on the extent to which
they feel positively or negatively motivated.
- **Openly Hostile**: I'll go out of my way to actively
  interfere with what you're doing, regardless of
  the risk and consequences to me.
- **Passive-Aggressive:** I'm not overtly against you,
  but I will cause unseen conflict and obstacles
  below the surface when the opportunity arises.

- **Neutral:** I'm undecided and don't feel strongly one way or another, so if what I do helps you fine, if it hurts you, that's fine too.
- **Compliant:** I'll do whatever I have to just to get you off my back and keep my job, following the letter of the law.
- **Cooperative:** I think what you are doing is valuable. I will help as my time and energy allows.
- **Committed:** I think working together is mutually beneficial, and I want to actively collaborate.
- **Actively Partnering:** I see my success as integrally tied to your success. I'll put myself on the line for you and expect you will do the same for me. We have a symbiotic relationship.

Remember, just because someone isn't openly hostile doesn't mean they are truly onboard. In order to move them toward the active partnership ideal for success, ensure you are positively motivating them with opportunities that directly correspond to their needs, whether sustenance, safety, community, or beyond.

Community
Many recreational poker players' needs reside at the community level. Whether it is to tell stories, have drinks, bond with friends, or blow off steam, they play poker more to play *with* their friends than *against* them. If you think of yourself as a poker player who is "too good" to play for social reasons, try this test:

The Social Player Test:
- Do you quit playing when there are only two or three people left in the game?
- When you play online, do you use chat?
- Has it been a long time since you arranged a heads-up poker game?
- When you play in public, do you take a friend or friends with you?

If you answered yes to one or more of these questions, then meeting your social needs is probably a significant driver behind your poker playing. There is nothing wrong with this. But remember, it's probably not coincidental that most recreational players want a social outlet <u>and</u> most recreational players don't win money. If you can make sure the people around you are having a good time - eating, drinking, and being merry - they will probably overlook the fact that they are losing money and providing an ongoing stream of funds.

Similarly, community is where many project team members' needs reside. Most people feel at least moderately safe and secure in their jobs and have their baseline necessities covered. Some of them then look to their jobs to provide social interaction and sense of community. Sharing funny emails, bonding around the water cooler, and having a few laughs over lunch can make or break the success of many workers' days.

One school of thought is to try to sanitize projects from these types of social activities because they waste valuable time. However, Maslow's hierarchy states that if people's community needs are not met, either on the job or in another setting, they cannot focus on higher goals, such as reaching the project's specified results. Therefore, a different philosophy is to try to structure the appropriate amount of community into the project to simultaneously meet both social and project needs. Some project tasks can be appropriately, or even optimally, planned as social events. Activities primarily energetic in nature, such as identifying likes and dislikes of a design, brainstorming potential marketing messages, and discovering hopes for the effort, are great candidates for community building in a relaxed, social environment. The activity doesn't have to be an extravagant outing. Something as simple as bringing in donuts to the conference room, holding the meeting in the cafeteria, or moving the discussion outside on a nice day, can improve the social dynamic without imposing on those who do not have high social needs.

Is it worthwhile to divert some of the precious project time, energy and funding to community building? For today's projects, the answer is: Absolutely. It is not just necessary to build community to help team members meet their social needs. It is necessary because community directly affects the bottom line. When people feel part of the same community, they communicate more effectively, and effective communication is crucial to success in the modern business world. David Weinberger and Christopher Locke, in *The Cluetrain Manifesto: The End of Business as Usual*, acknowledge the importance of communities and communication in business.

A knowledge worker is someone whose job entails having really interesting conversations. Conversations are where intellectual capital gets generated.

So, if you want ground breaking results that require leveraging the experience and visions of many people, you must establish an environment where they can effectively communicate.

The Impact of Community on Effectiveness
Turbo-charge effective communication by injecting two items: affinity and trust. Affinity, communication, and trust are interrelated in such a dynamic way that they rarely remain in a steady state. Either they are in a *virtuous* cycle creating a very high performing group or they are in a *vicious* cycle fostering fear, closed-doors, and disrespect. The following diagrams illustrate how these cycles start, feed back, and accelerate.
Virtuous cycle – The more people communicate, the more they trust each other. The more they trust each other, the more affinity they have for one another. The more they like each other, the more they communicate...and so on.

High Performing Group
Communication, Trust, and Affinity

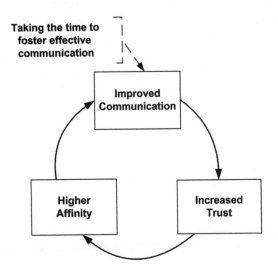

Vicious cycle – When something triggers a breach in trust, either intentionally or through a misunderstanding, people start to trust each other less. They then begin to like each other just a little less. Because their affinity has slipped, they communicate less. Once communication lessens, they begin to get more suspicious of one another. Then affinity degrades even further. If not stopped, this cycle will feed on itself and can quickly lead to degenerating affinity, communication, and trust...until the group is in complete dysfunction.

Breakdowns in Affinity, Communication and Trust

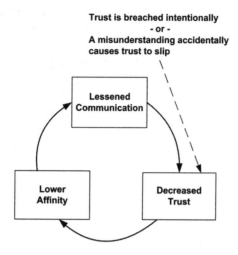

Trust is breached intentionally
- or -
A misunderstanding accidentally
causes trust to slip

If your organization or project team is in a vicious cycle of distrust, dislike, and ineffective communication, proactive steps are needed to break and reverse the pattern. Of these three elements, you can only directly impact one: communication. A team can't make a pact to all come in on Monday liking each other more, just as you can't send a memo telling everyone to trust each other more. These directives simply won't work. Therefore, the only direct, effective line of attack is to improve communication. If you want to enhance affinity and trust, start by improving the quality and quantity of communications.

The reason people are often so hostile to team-building or community-building activities is that the activities:

- Try to focus on affinity or trust directly rather than through communication.
- Fail to tie directly to what the team is trying to accomplish on their projects.

Activities such as Hawaiian shirt Friday, ice-cream bar socials, and taking turns falling back into each others arms are disliked not so much because they are lame (which they are) but because they are ineffective. They are ineffective because they are structured to try to directly improve affinity and trust rather than using communication to feed the communication-trust-affinity cycle. In planning and preparing activities to meet social needs, ensure the activities:

1. **Create outputs that advance the project.** People need to walk out with tangible results and see progress toward the project goals.
2. **Focus on two-way communication.** Provide a venue for people to be heard and feel listened to. The last thing people want is more time sitting around being preached at or talking past one another.

Be vigilant not to let the social aspect squeeze out all other needs. Also, be careful not to mix oil and water by taking activities that require detailed, difficult decision making and adding these to the Christmas party.

By following these guidelines for adding, in moderation, social activities, you can enhance communication channels and greatly increase the team's productivity for creating new ideas, overcoming obstacles, and generating intellectual capital.

Esteem

Want to win some easy money? If so, be on the lookout for poker players playing to impress others. It is not uncommon to see players try to "raise their game" because someone at the table is: their poker coach, a poker legend, or a potential mate. For people who have adequate sustenance, safety, and community in their lives, the need to impress can be a very strong force in driving decisions and actions. Just as a golfer can over-swing, and a salesperson oversell, poker players tend to over-impress with their play. This type of play typically backfires as they bluff at too many hands, fail to fold when they know they are beat, and make too many plays just to save face. This can quickly snowball as these decisions cost the player substantial chips early on, and they feel even that much more pressure to impress. Pretty quickly, they can over-impress their way to going broke.

On projects, stakeholders' need for esteem can be either a great motivator or, as in the poker example above, a great obstacle. For project participants who are driven by esteem, they are looking to be held in high regard by those whose recognition they care about. Establishing mechanisms to deliver this recognition serves as a strong motivator, as described by author John Richelsen:

Men can be stimulated to show off their good qualities to the leader who seems to think they have good qualities.

Creating this type of stimulation requires attention to six factors. First, make sure you know what "good qualities" means to an individual. Would they rather be seen as perfect, polished, smart, fun, or courageous? While some people want to be "polished and professional" others strive to be "entrepreneurial mad scientists". Praise for the first person would be criticism for the second person, and vice versa. Therefore, the admiration must match both the characteristics *they want* to be admired for and the behaviors *you want* (and need) for project success.

Next, know who they most want to be admired by. Is it you? (If not, why not, and can you do something about that?) Assuming you are on the list, who are the others? Your boss? Their boss? Other team members? The customer? The praise should come from those whose opinions count the most.

Third, know how to deliver the praise. Again, take the time to know your stakeholders. Some people want and need public recognition, while others hate to be publicly recognized but love individual praise. Therefore, customize how you will deliver the message to the specific needs of the individual. If they are a person who loves the limelight, acknowledge their achievements in a large meeting while they are present. If they are someone who detests the public eye, take the time to sit down with them face-to-face to tell them you truly are thankful and hold them in high regard for what they accomplish.

Next, praise needs to be sincere. For people craving esteem, faint or false praise is a huge de-motivator. In the 2004 World Series of Poker, after losing a particularly unlucky hand, Phil Hellmuth commented to his opponent: "nice hand, well played, you deserved it." ESPN announcer Norman Chad quickly explained what Phil really meant was: not a nice hand, not well played, you didn't deserve it. By using false praise, Phil was seemingly trying to influence his opponent into making poor future decisions (and probably make himself feel good, too). Always make sure your praise is credible to the individual receiving it or you risk it having a de-motivating effect.

The fifth element, timeliness, is critical because of the fleeting nature of emotion. Immediately after doing a good job, people internally feel their own success. External praise given at this point magnifies one's own feelings, doubling or tripling this positive emotion. If you wait until time passes and the individual's internal feelings are gone, you are multiplying by zero and your belated praise will have very little impact.

Finally, the praise should be specific and relate to behavior that you want to see again. Platitudes like "Super Job" and "Hooray for You" get tuned out. Pick a specific aspect to emphasize as you say thanks, e.g. "Thank you for the great work on the design. I am impressed you were able to precisely strike the critical balance between creativity and professionalism in a way that executives will embrace."

To help remember these six steps when trying to stimulate desired behaviors, use the following who, what, where, when, how, and why approach:

1. **Who** – Determine whose admiration the individual most desires. The praise should come from, or at least be seen by, those people.

2. **What** – Identify the characteristics the individual wants to be admired for and how those characteristics overlap with the behaviors you need for project success.
3. **Where** – Analyze whether the praise would be most effective if communicated publicly or privately – every person and situation is unique.
4. **When** – Make the praise timely, when it will amplify the recipient's own internal feelings about their success.
5. **How** – Ensure the praise is sincere or it will be demotivating.
6. **Why** – Praise the specific behaviors you want to see more of and that are required for project success.

Self-Actualization

The dictionary defines self-actualization as: "to fully reach one's potential." People who have their lower needs adequately met can focus on realizing their full potential. They then become driven by the need to create, explore, make a contribution to the world, and do the things they feel they were born to do.

If your poker opponent is self-actualizing, you need to assess if this self-actualization is enabling or detracting from their ability to win money. If your opponent feels they were born to be a poker champion and has invested the time to develop a mastery of the game, run away from the table, or better yet, retire to the rail to watch, study, and learn. If, on the other hand, they made a fortune in the internet boom and feel like poker is their outlet for creativity and exploration, let their chips explore their way over to your stack.

At work, seek out those team members who are not needy for social, community, and esteem but are ready to reach their full potential. For these team members, don't structure a job to make it easy and fail-safe. Make it as big, challenging, and self-actualizing as possible.

*I most seriously believe that one does people the best
service by giving them some elevating work to do and
thus indirectly elevating them.*
– Albert Einstein

Recapping Influencing People

Always remember project leadership, like poker, is a game of people. You must do your best with the cards you are dealt. Taking the time to analyze and care about those around you can provide the little bit of "luck" needed to draw a winning hand.

*People will forget what you said,
people will forget what you did,
but people will never forget how you made them feel.*
- Source unknown

BEATING THE ODDS

CHAPTER 8

Playing On-tilt:
Decision Making Is Based on Logic <u>and</u> Emotion

*If scientific reasoning were limited to the logical
processes of arithmetic, we should not get very far in
our understanding of the physical world. One might
as well attempt to grasp the game of poker entirely by
the use of the mathematics of probability.*
- Vannevar Bush, Godfather of the internet

Winning or losing in a poker game comes down to how
a few pivotal hands are played. Similarly, whether or not a
project succeeds is often the result of a small number of
crucial decisions. Successful project leaders are those who

know how to engage those around them to make not only high quality decisions, but high quality decisions that achieve ongoing, active support.

The first step in reaching these powerful decisions is to remember that people are people. People do not make decisions the same way a computer does - applying a formula to multiple, quantifiable factors and coming up with the same answer every time. For people, intellectual factors are just one part of the equation. Human decision making also occurs on an emotional axis. On the intellectual axis, one may have a lot of information, a little information, no information, or even incorrect information on which to base decisions. Similarly, on the emotional axis, one may have positive, negative, or perhaps, no feelings influencing decision making. To help people make high quality decisions that will stick, you need to prepare both their head and their heart. Make sure they *think* it is the right thing to do and that they *feel* good about the choice.

People Make Decisions on Two Axes

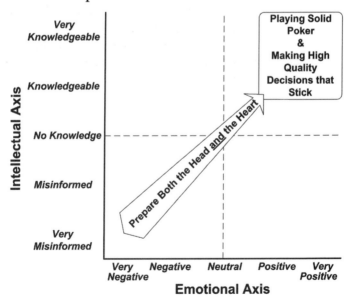

On-tilt Decision Making

Negative emotions can lead to bad decision making. A perfect example is when poker players go "on-tilt." On-tilt players are angry players whose emotions have gotten the better of them because of something that has happened at the table, at home, or at the office. They may have lost a big deal, gotten into a heated argument with someone they care about, or most commonly, lost a big hand on a bad-beat (where a weaker opponent with a weaker hand took down the pot thanks to a miracle card). While on-tilt, their emotions are so strong that even though they intellectually understand what they should do, they still do the opposite. Sometimes on-tilt players go so far as to go "all-in blind," pushing all of their chips into the center before the cards are even dealt, a purely emotional bet based on zero information. Perhaps worse than players who bet with no information, are on-tilt players who misread their cards because they are so angry they literally can't see straight. I have watched players lose huge pots because they thought they had A-K but really had 2-K, or thought they had a straight when they only had a four card straight. (If you think these players were on-tilt before the hand, you should have seen them after.)

The following illustration depicts the quality of decision making based on the poker player's intellectual and emotional conditions.

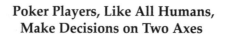

Poker Players, Like All Humans, Make Decisions on Two Axes

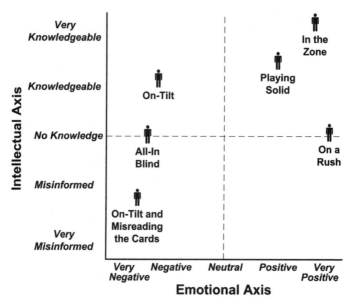

Decision Making at Work

Decision making on projects follows a similar pattern. When the decision is easy and low risk, people are often non-confrontational and will probably go along with the recommendations as long as they are positive on <u>either</u> of the two axes:

1. If they feel good about it but don't understand it, they will allow it to proceed in a wait and see mode.
2. Similarly, if they understand it, but don't particularly like it, they will get on board, albeit hesitantly.

However, for those key decisions requiring risk and sacrifice from the participants, you need to ensure that they are strongly positive on <u>both</u> the intellectual and emotional axes. To enable your stakeholders to commit to a difficult decision, start by identifying on the intellectual axis their position in regard to the situation.

- Are they knowledgeable, understanding why the decision needs to be made and what the options are for moving ahead?
- Are they misinformed or confused about what is being proposed?
- Are they at zero, knowing next to nothing about the situation?

Then, look at their emotional state:
- Are they feeling positive and excited about what they are being asked to support?
- Are they negative, having been burned by something similar in the past, anxious about the risk, or fearful for other emotional reasons?
- Are they neutral, not caring much about this one way or the other?

Like poker players, project decision makers move in and out of many different modes depending on their intellectual and emotional states.

Common Decision Making Modes

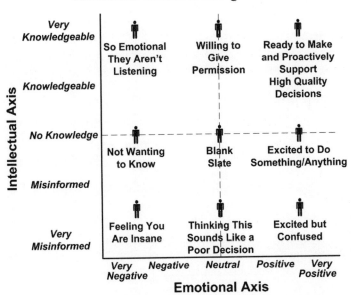

Preparing Stakeholders to Make and Support High Quality Decisions

In order to facilitate high quality decision making that will have lasting support, as project leaders, we must ensure that people are *prepared* to make and support those decisions. If someone doesn't understand the situation and has negative feelings toward the recommendation, we must help them become more positive on both axes.

Preparing Stakeholders to Make and Support High Quality Decisions

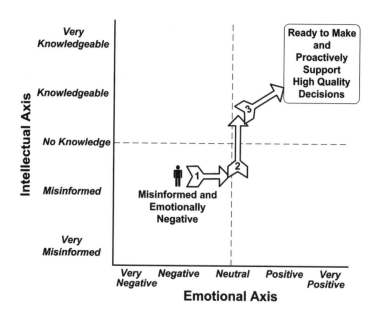

Helping people move intellectually and helping them move emotionally are two distinctly different tasks. If your audience is both emotionally and intellectually negative, to ready them for difficult decision making, I recommend a three step approach.

1. Begin by working on the emotional axis because people who are feeling angry or fearful usually aren't capable of listening clearly enough to be moved intellectually, no matter how detailed your case or how loud you yell.
2. Once they are emotionally ready to listen, only then, begin to educate them on the facts of the problem and the pros and cons of potential solutions.
3. Bolster the staying power of the decision by elaborating on the facts of the situation and helping them feel positively energized about the recommendation before a final decision is made.

Diffusing people's emotional negativity requires active listening on your part, rather than a lot of talking. Help people vent and feel they are being heard. A terrific way to demonstrate to someone that you're listening and hearing them is to write down what they're saying. If you do nothing else, pull out a piece of paper, or better yet, a flipchart and say: "I want to make sure I understand your hopes and fears around what we are trying to accomplish." If you focus on listening and writing their thoughts in big letters it:

- Helps establish that you care about them.
- Helps them settle down. If what they are saying is wild or nonsensical, seeing it written down on paper will help them tone down their exaggerations and clarify their true thoughts.
- Makes them feel served.
- Most importantly, helps ensure a higher quality decision. When people are upset, most of the time, they have a valid and important insight into the situation. Your goal is not just to calm them down so they will agree with you; rather, you want to find the cause of their emotional concern and leverage it in formulating a solution.

By allowing your stakeholders to vent and be heard, they will then become emotionally ready to listen to you and able to think about the decision logically. You then can help them make an informed decision by presenting a logical business case for what needs to be decided.

> *Seek first to understand and then to be understood.*
> - Stephen R. Covey, *The 7 Habits of Highly Effective People*

Where do the intellectual arguments for this case come from? From your stakeholder analysis that identifies the overlap between the stakeholder's needs and the project's needs. Explain how the decision logically works to accomplish both. If you only focus on educating them on how the decision meets the organization's goals, they might grant you *permission* to proceed. But if you can show them how it simultaneously helps them meet their goals, they will provide *active support* as the project proceeds.

To secure their active support, once they agree that the suggested decision sounds logical, readdress their emotional feelings regarding it. Focus on those things that energize them; the things that cause them to get out of bed at 5AM; the things that when discussed trigger them to put down their Blackberry and actually listen. It is only by addressing these needs that your stakeholders will put themselves on the line for the project.

Exercise: Assessing Decision Making Readiness
Try your hand at assessing people's readiness to make high quality decisions. Consider in which quadrant the following individuals would fall on the intellectual and emotional axes, and map your assessment on the template below:

- Christina, who is emotionally on board but misunderstands the approach.
- George, who knows it is the right thing to do but got burned last time.

- Mary, who has no preconceived notions or feelings because she is totally in the dark.
- David, who is mad about the plan because he has been accidentally misinformed about how it will work.
- Annie, who understands and loves the idea.

Decision Making Readiness Template

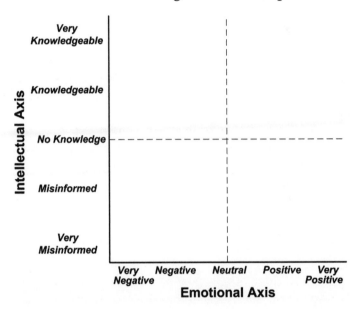

119

Your assessment of each individual's decision making readiness should look something like the following:

Decision Making Readiness

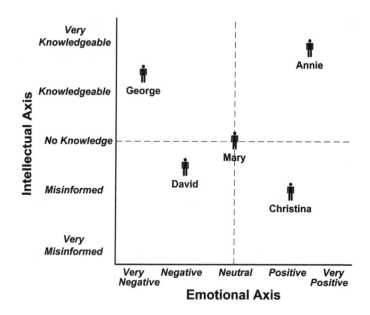

As you can see, Annie is the only stakeholder who is in the ideal state to make an intellectually informed decision that she will both think is correct and be excited about supporting. George and David, both emotionally negative regarding the decision must first, at a minimum, get to an emotionally neutral state before they will accept the decision. David, Mary and Christina all need more information about the proposed decision before they can intellectually understand and therefore, support it.

Exercise: Identifying Strategies for Gaining Support

Now that you understand where each stakeholder is, how do you get them to where you need them to be?

Based on the stakeholder analysis below, identify at least two strategies you might suggest for David, Christina, and Mary to motivate them to become win-win active partners.

Motivating Strategies Template

Project end results: More sales to new customers

Stakeholder (and Role)	Individual Goal	"Win-win" Motivational Strategy
David (Team Member)	Exposure to executives.	
Christina (Team Member)	Chance to travel.	
Mary (Project Sponsor)	Show that she's an innovator.	

While there is no single right or wrong answer for these, your strategies may look something like the following:

Sample Motivating Strategies

Project end results:　More sales to new customers

Stakeholder (and Role)	Individual Goal	"Win-win" Motivational Strategy
David (Team Member)	Exposure to executives.	• Assign to work with the CEO on major sales calls. • Allow to present at the executive steering committee.
Christina (Team Member)	Chance to travel.	• Suggest she volunteer to lead the vendor road show. • Allow her to lead focus groups with European customers.
Mary (Project Sponsor)	Show that she's an innovator.	• Where appropriate, choose leading edge technology. • Work with her to co-write an article for the business press that simultaneously highlights her accomplishments and the attractiveness of your new product.

A Minute to Learn and a Lifetime to Master

While the lessons of Chapters 7 and 8 are based in common sense, they can take years to truly master. Don't get frustrated by trying to implement it all perfectly tomorrow. Rather, to get started, focus on three basics:

1. Identify and prioritize the key stakeholders whose support you need and who must be influenced for the project to be successful.
2. Using a napkin, flipchart, or any piece of paper, draw the intellectual and emotional axes and plot each individual's current state in regard to the project and decision to be made.
3. For those who are not positive on both axes, take the time to:
   • Listen to them about their emotional issues.
   • Allow them to inform you on what is needed from their perspective.
   • Educate them on the decision by talking in terms of the things that they care about, i.e. how the decision will be win-win for them and the organization.
   • Continue to promote to them the overlap between the project's goals and their passions.

Remember, as in poker, where going home at night a winner or loser will come down to how a few pivotal hands are played, project success often depends on how a few key decisions are made. Your success as a project leader hinges on your ability to engage those around you to not only make high quality decisions, but high quality decisions that receive ongoing, active support. Therefore:

Before you try to satisfy "the client,"
understand and satisfy the person.
– Harry Beckwith, *Selling the Invisible*

BEATING THE ODDS

CHAPTER 9

Establishing House Rules:
The Secret of a Well Run Game

Jack McCall killed Wild Bill Hickock because
he thought he had been <u>cheated</u> out of a
twenty-five cent pot (he probably had been).
- Ken Warren, *Winner's Guide to Texas Hold 'Em Poker*

You don't get shot by another poker player for playing smart and taking their money. You get shot at the poker table for breaking the rules of the game.

So how do you avoid breaking the rules and getting shot? First, don't assume that just because you're playing Texas hold 'em everyone is playing by the same rules.

From house to house, cardroom to cardroom, online site to online site, there are different formal <u>and</u> informal rules players are expected to follow. For instance, when you sit down to a game, you should know:

- Is check-raising expected and accepted, allowed but considered a breach of etiquette, or not allowed?
- Do the cards "speak for themselves" or must players state what they think they have and live by that call?
- Are string bets (reaching back into your stack for more chips) illegal, allowed but frowned upon, or freely permitted?
- Is talking about your cards during play, even if you have folded, accepted, okay as long as you are lying, or will it get you kicked out of the game?
- Will answering your cell phone at the table cause your cards to be folded automatically, or, is it no big deal?

Avoid unnecessary, distracting confrontations (emotional or physical) by ensuring that there is a clear set of rules and norms for your game that are accepted by everyone. Although it is tempting and easy to assume everyone knows the rules by which you are playing, remember the adage: when you assume you make an ASS out of U and ME.

Although I haven't seen any punches thrown, I certainly have seen ruffled feathers and hurt feelings. When things have gotten heated, almost universally it was because of a value clash over the rules of the game. What one person sees as a shrewd and clever move, the other sees as an immoral, cheap trick. Unfortunately, once tempers flare, it is usually too late to resolve the dispute without creating an emotional winner and loser. Not only does the loser lose the pot, they resent being judged as wrong.

Avoiding this type of confrontation is why poker rooms have a list of rules posted at every table and why you should, too. If you think it is too geeky to laminate a list for your home, at least verbally review the rules before playing in order to head off potential problems. By preventing these problems, you can help everyone focus on the reasons they came, as well as have more fun.

In business, there are house rules as well. The principles that govern and guide both the project approach and the implementation of the end results often are referred to as the project's values. As with poker, most people want to assume that they are already on the same page rather than "waste" the time to talk through and write down the principles governing the project. Once issues arise and things get heated, it is too late to resolve the project house rules without picking a winner and creating a loser.

So what are these house rules that will guide how we play the game on our projects? They come in two primary flavors:

1. **Optimizing Values** – These *trade-off priorities* are chosen to help the organization best meet its goals. These values carry with them virtually no moral connotation. They simply answer the question: what trade-offs will we take when we *can't have it all* to ensure the team is acting in harmony in reaching its results. Optimizing values typically include the classic trade-off between speed, cost, focus, and quality.

2. **Regulating Values** – These values *impede the project* from moving as quickly, cheaply, broadly, and to the quality levels that would otherwise be possible. The organization often chooses these costly values for strong moral, cultural, or other beliefs. Examples of regulating values include: abiding the law, having integrity, or practicing eco-friendliness. These values may impede the project's progress and limit its options but the organization is willing to pay that price to do what it considers the "right" thing.

The chosen values may vary widely from project to project, depending on the environment, goals, and personalities involved. They do not exist in a vacuum. They are influenced by enterprise principles, the organizational unit's culture, the project's goals, individual team members' beliefs, customers' needs, and other factors. Therefore, you need to be clear on the values and tradeoffs for **each specific project**.

The following template identifies a starter set of six areas where value conflicts most commonly arise. Review them with project participants to determine the desired balance for each specific project. Make sure to reach agreement **before conflict arises** by sitting down the first week to determine what is expected for the effort. Document the choice by circling the agreed to target.

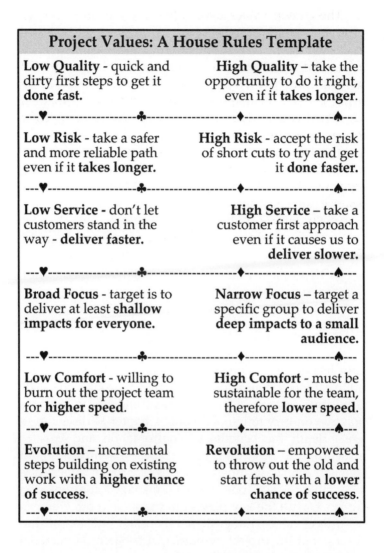

Project Values: A House Rules Template	
Low Quality - quick and dirty first steps to get it **done fast**.	**High Quality** – take the opportunity to do it right, even if it **takes longer**.
---♥-------------------♣-------------------♦-------------------♠---	
Low Risk - take a safer and more reliable path even if it **takes longer**.	**High Risk** - accept the risk of short cuts to try and get it **done faster**.
---♥-------------------♣-------------------♦-------------------♠---	
Low Service - don't let customers stand in the way - **deliver faster**.	**High Service** – take a customer first approach even if it causes us to **deliver slower**.
---♥-------------------♣-------------------♦-------------------♠---	
Broad Focus - target is to deliver at least **shallow impacts for everyone**.	**Narrow Focus** – target a specific group to deliver **deep impacts to a small audience**.
---♥-------------------♣-------------------♦-------------------♠---	
Low Comfort - willing to burn out the project team for **higher speed**.	**High Comfort** - must be sustainable for the team, therefore **lower speed**.
---♥-------------------♣-------------------♦-------------------♠---	
Evolution – incremental steps building on existing work with a **higher chance of success**.	**Revolution** – empowered to throw out the old and start fresh with a **lower chance of success**.
---♥-------------------♣-------------------♦-------------------♠---	

Why do this in a group? Through the act of sitting down together to define the rules of the game, stakeholders bond as a team and form a partnership for the good of the project and the business.

Why is nailing down values crucial to project success? While it is natural for sponsors and customers to want it all, many of these principles conflict with one another. Therefore, prioritizing and then *documenting* the expected and accepted trade-offs together is a necessity to prevent misunderstandings and wasted effort. In the absence of an agreed upon, written set of rules, each participant in the effort will rely on their own personal value set. You can be sure friction will result. Project value clashes can become deeply emotional and personal, often resembling a political or religious argument. While there is arguably no "right" or "wrong" side to a political or religious debate, by coming together to establish project specific values, your organization is saying the values:

- Define what is *right* for *this project*.
- Delineate the behaviors the company is willing to pay for.
- Determine what will guide us in making efficient and consistent decisions.
- Override individual preferences.

Is Confrontation Bad?

So, what's wrong with a little confrontation? Maybe a little heated discussion would give us the adrenaline needed to get focused and push through? Confrontation can be a positive force in poker, business, and life to get to a solution on very tough decisions. Chapter 11 discusses in great depth the benefits of confrontation and how to structure it to produce positive business returns without damaging relationships. In terms of project values, it is preferable to have one big, well-managed confrontation up front, with the key players in the same room who can set project values, rather than a thousand little skirmishes throughout the project by participants based on personal values.

Personal Values vs. Project Values

When concrete and difficult choices about what is right and wrong for the project are made, there is the potential for individual project members to have personal beliefs so in conflict with the project values that they should remove themselves (or in even more extreme situations, be removed) from the project. Otherwise their constant confrontation with the accepted rules will bring productivity to a halt at every critical decision or action.

Establishing Agreement and Accountability

The following four tips can help you make project values an effective and useable tool in your organization:

1. If key decision makers are turned off by the term project "values," perceiving values as too touchy-feely a subject to merit business time and discussion, refer to project values by another name. Instead of requesting time to prioritize project values, schedule a meeting to establish the house rules needed to ensure everyone is playing the same game. If that still isn't machismo enough, try saying: "We need rules of engagement so we can charge ahead at full speed while avoiding unintended and unacceptable collateral damage."

2. If people still resist taking the time to collaboratively develop project values, draft what you think are the best project values given the current situation of the effort. Publicize them as a draft, letting everyone know you plan to use them to guide your actions and decisions. Encourage others to disagree and iterate the list together. The nudge of a draft often triggers discussions leading to getting the house rules in order.

3. Monitor the project to ensure participants live up to the stated values. People may not respect the project's values if no one watches to see if they are being followed. If you create a list of values on the first week but it is immediately put on the shelf to gather dust, people will revert to their personal value set and be destined for conflict. Make ensuring that values are being followed a routine part of leading the project. When making

assignments, you can reinforce the project's values by discussing what these values mean to the particular assignment, e.g. "Our project values say that quality is high, so if it is going to take you longer than assigned to do a quality job, let me know as soon as possible so I can adjust our schedule." You don't have to literally measure the values in terms of a quantifiable number, but you should be able to observe trends in individual behavior and behavior across the project that suggests the values are sticking. It is especially important to monitor the regulating values that slow the speed of the project to ensure they are not being sacrificed in order to stay on schedule.

4. Lead by example. Nothing is worse than a hypocrite harping on and on about values. If you want people to follow the values, start by living them yourself, showing the way to doggedly reach results while still abiding by the accepted rules of the game.

A Real World Aside: As I wrote this chapter, I had the following email exchange with my good friend, BC. Although a bit of a tangent, BC so perfectly hit the topics of living up to your values and leading by example, that I was compelled to include it here.

From: John Schroeder
To: 'BC'
Subject: Business Card

I got a business card from a business that helps people get organized. The bottom read: National Association of Professional Organizers. I was curious, so I went to their website and saw that coming up is the: NAPO Annual National Conference & Organizing Expo in Boston.

I signed us up to go, it should be a blast because I bet those Professional Organizers know how to Par-tay.

From: BC
To: 'John Schroeder'
Subject: RE: Business Card

That better be the most well-organized party ever. You need to take whatever criteria they give you on how to organize your work schedule/life/whatever, and see if they practice what they preach when the rubber hits the yellow-brick road. All meetings starting on time? Information, schedules and logistics at your finger tips?? No delays because they are out of supplies, forgot the long extension cord, or the projection unit sucks???

See... at the school I work in, teachers don't do that. We had a big "in-service" meeting the other day, which means that all the teachers have to listen to the vice principals go through the district-

mandated stuff and talk about blah, blah, blah.
It's boring, but you still need to respect them and
everything, right? Noooo. The teachers act just
like the kids in their classrooms. There were
groups of people talking quietly, but loudly
enough so that people around them couldn't hear
what was being said. And they all complained
about having to go to the "stupid meeting" in the
first place. A lot of them act exactly like the kids
they complain about in their classes. "Kids these
days don't pay attention. They don't *respect* me
when I'm up there trying to give them a better
education, etc., etc." But when put in the same
situation, a lot of the same teachers do exactly
the same thing.

I say it all the time: words are worthless. People
respond by actions. Take a lazy guy and put him
in an environment of hard-working, likable people
and there's a good chance he'll step up. Take a
hard-working guy and put him in an environment
of lazy slackers and there's a good chance he
might say "screw it...everyone else is lazy, why
should I work so hard when I know I can't do it
alone?" Same with project managers. You want
your people to work hard? You work hard. You
want people to be open-minded? You be open-
minded. You want people to be able to take criticism for their ideas/concepts/etc.? You take criticism for your actions, and show your team members how to handle it like a professional.

My last company had Core Values, and right now
I can't even name them. But when I worked
there, I didn't need to know how to recite them for
a class. The people there (most of them anyway)
actually lived and worked that way. It was inher-
ent in the way they spoke, walked, shook your
hand, listened to you, ran a meeting, went to

lunch, whatever. Sure, you can write it down, but the guy on the ground at the client site in Winnipeg isn't checking the Intranet each day to see what his Core Values are. He does what the other guys on his/her team does, and does what his leadership does.

Those crazy African ants don't build those 30ft mounds of rhino dung because it was written down in their project plan. And hyenas don't chase down wounded antelopes because it was in their pack's mission statement. Some little hyena saw the other guys doing it and thought, "Hell, I can do that. I've got teeth and I can run. I need to get me some of that tasty antelope." Animals do that because they see others doing it. People are the same way, be it 3 year old kids, high school teachers, or project managers. **They hear what you say, but do what you do**.

Leading the Charge

To summarize the importance of project values:
- Are they worth it? Absolutely.
- Does it take a lot of effort to get them properly set up on day one? Certainly.
- Will the project benefit? Guaranteed.

Finally, if you're going to be a revolutionary and push this critical concept into your organization, make sure you're first in line, leading by example.

BEATING THE ODDS

PART 3

Shuffle Up and Deal

*Texas hold 'em is two hours of boredom
and 20 seconds of terror.*
– Jack McClelland, Bellagio Tournament Director

*Whenever you see a successful business,
someone once made a courageous decision.*
– Peter Drucker

BEATING THE ODDS

CHAPTER 10

I Knew I Should Have Folded:
The Importance of Discipline

*You cannot survive without that intangible quality we
call heart. If you win for thirty days in a row, that
makes no difference if on the thirty-first you have a bad
night, go crazy, and throw it all away.*
- Bobby Baldwin, 1978 World Series of Poker champion

When I first started playing Texas hold 'em, the
moments before the showdown - when the cards would be
flipped over and the winner revealed - brought back mem-
ories of Christmas morning. The anticipation for what the
future held was intense. I had no real feel for whether I
would be the winner or the loser. It was an exciting myst-

ery, like the game show *Let's Make a Deal*, where the contestants could keep the prize they had already won, or trade it in for what was behind "Door Number Three." While sometimes the curtain revealed a brand new car, just as often the contestants were crushed to learn they had traded a good prize for garbage.

As I gained experience, the showdown started to lose much of its magical quality. I began to be able to predict, with a surprising degree of accuracy, whether or not I was going to be the winner or the loser before the cards were even turned over. The act of flipping the cards simply confirmed what I already "knew" – what I could feel in my gut.

Once I developed the ability to predict if I had the winner or the loser, I thought I would start winning significant money playing poker. I was dead wrong. Developing this ability was certainly significant, but there was a second, and equally crucial, piece missing if I was to reach my desired outcomes:

Once you learn to <u>hear</u> your gut,
You must still learn to <u>obey</u> your gut.

It isn't until you learn the discipline to actually fold when you know you have the worse hand (even if it is three aces), or bet strongly on the river when you have the best hand (even if it is only a pair of deuces), that your results will start to improve.

Chapters 2 through 9 of this book focused on setting up projects for success by having:
1. Agreement on the desired end results;
2. Adaptable plans;
3. Dedicated resources;
4. Sufficient time to play your game; and
5. A focus on people.

However, simply *knowing* these fundamentals does not ensure success. *They must be acted upon.*

As mentioned in the preface, I had several working papers and speeches on project leadership, including: *What Training for a Marathon Teaches Us about Project Management, Dieting Fundamentals for Project Leadership,* and *Everything I Need to Know about Leadership, I Learned from My Dog.*

In each case, no matter what analogy was used, the core message remained the same:

Knowing what to do is not enough.
The key to success is having the discipline to do it.

Training for a marathon is not a complex task, but it does require discipline. You cannot wing it when you are talking about running 26 miles. You actually have to put the time and energy into the training miles, week after week. There is no miracle formula except: no pain, no gain. If you run five miles every other day this week, you will be ready to run six miles next week. Simply repeat and increase as necessary. So, if you understand the marathon training process, are you ready to put on your shoes and run 26 miles? No - of course not. You have to actually get out there and do the training week after week. Cramming at the last minute simply will not work for this type of effort.

Dieting works the same way. When it hits me that I need to lose 10 pounds, do I need to go out and learn more about metabolism, net-carbs versus regular-carbs, the new food pyramid, the glycemic index, etc.? No. I simply need to have the follow through to do the things that have worked for me in the past, such as - if it tastes good, spit it out.

In regard to discipline, all of these activities – dieting, running a marathon, project leadership, and poker – are very similar. You simply can't make up for periods of lax discipline. You must consistently stay focused for the entire effort.

However, project leadership and poker are far more challenging because they are far more complex. It is this combination of complexity <u>and</u> discipline that makes these

141

endeavors so difficult. But it also makes successful results so satisfying, and the salaries, for people who have proven they can consistently deliver, so much higher.

**The Complex and Disciplined Nature
of Poker and Project Leadership**

	High Complexity	Low Complexity
High Discipline	**I. Professional** • Winning at poker • Leading projects and people	**II. No Pain No Gain** • Training for a marathon • Dieting
Low Discipline	**III. Complicated Yet Casual** • Brainstorming marketing messages • Doing a crossword puzzle	**IV. Wing It** • Deciding where to go for lunch • Deciding what to wear to a sales call

How often do poker players come up short on discipline? All the time. Virtually every poker game I play in, someone will lose a big hand and say afterward: "I knew I should have folded, but I just couldn't bring myself to do it." The same is true when talking to business leaders about troubled projects. They will admit they *knew* what they needed to do to stay out of trouble but, for one reason or another, they *chose* a different path - often one that was less disciplined or less complex. In fact, many times they will echo the dejected poker players, saying, "I knew I should have taken the time to get that executive on board, but I just didn't do it."

So how do we improve our discipline? How can we have consistent and reliable follow-through to do what we *know* needs to be done?

One technique that is so basic and fundamental, yet so rarely done is to write things down. Putting pen to paper (or key to PC) helps successful project leaders:
- Be honest with themselves.
- Think through their decision making.
- Ensure they aren't just rationalizing bad decisions.

The power of writing things down is why, throughout this book, the advice is consistent: grab a piece of paper, even if it is a napkin, and take the time to write it down. Write down the results, write down the plan, write down the assessment of resources, write down the stakeholder analysis, etc.

A more specific instrument that helps with discipline is a project worry log. A worry log is a written document containing the things that could go wrong on the project, the things that could go better than expected on the project, and the things you feel are most crucial to project success. It does not need to be a complicated spreadsheet, but it should contain at least three elements:
1. What you are worried about.
2. Your strategy for dealing with the worry.
3. What you need to do immediately – if anything.

#	(1) What I Am Worried About	(2) Strategy for Moving Forward	(3) Immediate Next Steps
	Sample Napkin Project Worry Log		
1	The new VP does not seem fully onboard with the effort.	Understand her hopes for the effort, and do something at least once/week to promote our progress.	Schedule lunch with her next week to discuss.
2	We may be able to get some bonus funding since it is the end of the fiscal year.	Create a business case for why this project needs the surplus funds.	None. Revisit in 4 weeks.
3	Our team may be getting burned out.	Ensure the pace of the project is appropriate given the length of the schedule.	Do a quick assessment with the team to gauge the current status.

Why do you need to write these things down? Because projects are complex, and leadership requires discipline. You need a way to get all the ideas and concerns that are swimming around in your head out, so you can effectively focus on the task at hand.

Think of your worry log as a kind of:
"TiVo for project planning."
You no longer have to deal with everything the second it pops into your head - or on someone else's schedule.

To successfully use a project worry log, it must be much more like TiVo and nothing at all like an unreliable VCR. It must be trustworthy, at your finger tips, and able to provide exactly the information you want. This allows you to deal with worries on *your* schedule - when you can block the time and attention needed to focus on them.

Maintaining a project worry log helps you avoid:
- Trying to carry too much in your head, and becoming so overwhelmed that you do nothing well.
- Losing track, or completely forgetting ideas, risks, and tasks that are critical to success.
- Developing such a short attention span that you are never able to finish one thing before switching to another.
- Not being able to go home at night because you feel the weight of the world on your shoulders.

The act of writing your worries down helps you to make a commitment to yourself. It helps minimize the chance that you will be the one coming back and saying: "I knew we needed to get the new VP on board but..." or, "I assumed that was taken care of but..." or, "I guess I just totally dropped the ball on that."

Blocking time to specifically work on your worry log will increase your ability to actually do what you know needs to be done. Review the worry log and ask:
1. Have I followed through on the strategies and next steps I laid out?
2. If not, do I think it is because I have the wrong strategy? Or, have I lacked the discipline to do what I know needs to be done?
3. What else is on the horizon that could become a showstopper if I don't take action?

There is nothing fun or sexy about keeping a worry log, writing it down, and blocking time to work on it. I readily admit the disciplined approach is rarely the most fun approach.

If you're in Atlantic City and your desired end results are to gamble, drink, and socialize, a disciplined approach will not fit your needs. However, when you are on the job and leading a project funded by others, your responsibility is to create value for the organization.

While having fun can be a great side-benefit, the imperative to consistently deliver business results necessitates a disciplined approach.

Do something every day that you don't want to do; this is the golden rule for acquiring the habit of doing your duty.
- Mark Twain

CHAPTER 11

No Guts, No Glory:
Long-term Success Requires Courage

In poker, one must have courage: the courage to bet, to back one's convictions, one's intuitions, one's understanding. There can be no victory without courage.
David Mamet, author of *Glengarry Glen Ross*

All the plans, resources, time, people, and discipline in the world won't add up to sustained results if you don't have courage. On the job, at the table, and throughout your career, you must decide where you want to be:

You can be comfortable or outstanding, but not both.
You can't win big by playing it safe.
- Sally Hogshead, author of *Radical Careering*

Said another way: Are you playing *to win* or are you playing *not to lose*? While losing may be the opposite of winning, playing not to lose is a far cry from playing to win. The two opposing strategies are summed up in the following quotes:

Fortune favors		*When I grow up, I*
the bold.	vs.	*wanna be a yes man.*
- Virgil		- Monster.com commercial

In poker, there is a term for "yes men," those players who are content letting others make all the hard decisions. They are referred to as "calling stations" because they follow someone else's lead, call way too many bets when they are weak, and fail to raise when they are strong. What is the result of this type of play? Stacks of money wasted on hands that never had any real chance of winning and golden opportunities squandered for only minimal returns.

"Working stiff" is to business what calling station is to poker. Project leaders are in constant danger of falling into a calling station routine when they are neither actively pushing the action nor rigorously mucking low value activities. They simply go with the flow. Sometimes this behavior results from a work environment where they are so understaffed, overworked, and minimally empowered that they struggle just to keep their heads above water. Other times, due to a desire to try to prove they can do everything and please everyone, they quickly agree to every suggestion that comes across their desk. Regardless of the underlying causes, what these leaders fail to internalize is that:

Project leadership, like poker, is not for the timid.
Success on the job comes down to the ability to lead,
and successful leadership comes down to
the ability to have courage.

148

This is not meant to imply that you need to be ultra-aggressive, cut-throat, or take unnecessary risks to be a successful project leader. What it does say is that success requires you to have the courage to make hard choices and to insist that those around you also make hard choices. Making the tough calls is at the essence of what poker playing, project leadership, and this book are all about. In poker, if you are afraid to raise, you will never maximize the value of good cards. If you are afraid to fold, you will throw away too much money on losing bets. If you are afraid to bluff, you will only be as good as the cards you are dealt.

Making tough choices magnifies performance at the table and on the job. When answered correctly, hard choices transform a good opportunity into enormous returns. Of course, these results do not come without risk. Making the wrong call can quickly turn a golden opportunity into a whopping loss. Poker and projects are both subject to the premise of the risk/return ratio: the more you risk, the more you stand to gain <u>and</u> the more you stand to lose. Don't let the risk of loss scare you. If you are dissatisfied with the mediocre returns you are generating in business (or at the poker table):

Increase the risk and potential reward you are willing to accept by making <u>more</u> hard choices.

Admittedly, on rare occasions playing not to lose might be a fitting strategy. If you are killing time in the cardroom, waiting for your friends so you can go out on the town, a low risk, nothing gained, nothing lost approach to poker might be just right. Similarly, if your project at work is inconsequential and no one cares about its success; or, if all you care about is cashing your paycheck or building your resume, maybe you should be a yes man. In these cases, the strategies in this book do <u>not</u> apply to you. The discipline and courage *Beating the Odds* promotes is intended for projects that are mission critical, for projects that drive the economic well being of your company, and for projects that will make those around you less frustrated and more productive. When those around you are counting on your ability to win, and win big, the courage to make hard decisions becomes a necessity.

> *It doesn't matter how many times you fail.*
> *It doesn't matter how many times you almost*
> *get it right. No one is going to know or care about*
> *your failures, and neither should you. All that*
> *matters in business is that you get it right once.*
> *Then everyone can tell you how lucky you are.*
> - Mark Cuban, founder of Broadcast.com

On projects of importance, we must play to win. For that, courage is needed across the board:

- **Courage** to push beyond what people initially ask for, and to insist on an agreement connecting desired results to business outcomes.
- **Courage** to throw out an accepted and popular plan because it no longer matches reality, and to force a decision: "Are we going to keep deluding ourselves, or are we going to come up with a new plan that is honest and realistic?"
- **Courage** to be truthful to yourself and others in assessing if you have the resources needed to be successful - and to speak up immediately when you don't.
- **Courage** to say "No!" in order to focus your time and attention on the most crucial needs of the project, and not let urgent fires drive everything of long-term importance out of your day.
- **Courage** to engage people and to focus on meeting their needs in unison with the project's needs.
- **Courage** to discipline yourself to do what you know needs to be done, rather than doing what is comfortable.

So enough of Dilbert, that whining little weasel. When's the last time he pushed back? When's the last time he actually fought for an idea? He deserves what he gets. The age of revolution requires revolutionaries.
- Gary Hamel, *Leading the Revolution*

The Resolution to Succeed
Courage, in *Beating the Odds,* means two things:
- **Bold** – willingness to act in spite of the danger; and
- **Resolute** – determined to achieve the end results.

Why are there over a hundred references in this book to identifying, specifying, agreeing to, and writing down the desired results of your project? Because without those ends driving and guiding everything you do, you cannot be resolute; and without resolution, you cannot be courageous. As my brother Matt says: "It doesn't take courage to bluff someone, it only takes a few beers."

**While we must be bold,
the boldness must be born of purpose.**

At work, we must be business driven, with a laser-like focus on specified *business* results. If you take bold action just to be bold, you aren't being courageous, you're just being aggressive. If you take bold action just to try to beat someone else, you aren't being courageous, you're being competitive. If you take bold action just to intimidate others, you aren't being courageous, you're just being a jerk. It is only through *boldness to deliver on business results* that we are courageous.

In *Good to Great,* one of the best selling business books of all time, Jim Collins and his research team set out on a quantitative study of companies to get beyond all of the conventional wisdom, folklore, and urban legends in order to see what really makes companies successful. The data revealed that at the top of every good to great company was a leader embodying a combination of humility and will. Jim Collins refers to these executives as Level 5 Leaders:

151

Level 5 leaders display a compelling modesty, are self-effacing and understated...Level 5 leaders are fanatically driven, infected with an incurable need to produce sustained results...They are ambitious, to be sure, but ambitious first and foremost for the company, not themselves.

When you and your stakeholders invest the time to build consensus regarding the results of the effort, you have done far more than create "buy-in" and a mission statement to put on a coffee mug. Together, you have created more than an opportunity for Level 5 leadership. The group has issued a license to be bold and you now have an obligation to do what it takes to deliver success.

Carrying a license to be bold is a powerful thing but it does not give you license to kill, nor does it convey any kind of diplomatic immunity. So while you have a license for boldness, you must structure your approach for sustainable success, play within the rules of the game, and act with the humility and graciousness to help those around you to succeed.

Setting Up Productive Conflict

Long-term courageousness, as opposed to short-term bravado, requires setting up a context for *conflict* rather than *contest*. A contest is a zero-sum event where there is a winner and a loser, like a poker game between two players who only care about winning money. Conflict, on the other hand, can be structured for win-win resolution. Setting up positive conflict requires:

1. **The ability to pick your battles** – making sure the ends justify the means and that the bold step is worth taking for you, the project, and your "opponent."
2. **Proactively triggering action** – confronting the issue head-on rather than waiting for the action to come to you.
3. **Structuring a positive confrontation** – ensuring the encounter has the elements required for business success, rather than a clash of egos.

- **Vision** – understanding the expected business results of the project and ensuring you believe in, and are able to communicate effectively, the importance of those results.
- **Rules of engagement** – making certain every one agrees to and abides by the same project values, the house rules for the project.
- **Emotional readiness** – focusing on what is needed for business success, not seeking revenge, saving face, or stoking egos.

Putting these prerequisites in place enables you and the project's stakeholders to act boldly in resolving the group's differences, enabling the participants to reach consensus in finding the best answers. Today's projects require consensus because it often takes a wide, voluntary following to create breakthrough results. Don't avoid confrontation with these stakeholders and thus, compromise on a solution everyone is equally dissatisfied with. Structure confrontation to leverage the diversity of experiences and opinions, to find an optimal solution that all participants believe is the best way to proceed given the constraints of the situation.

Without conflict, there can never be true consensus.
- Abe Wong, founder of Advanced Strategies, Inc.

Pick Your Battles Wisely

Question whether a painful battle is worth fighting. Battles worth fighting are those that will systemically alter the path of the project and enhance the probability of success. You don't need to be bold in arguing about which kind of pizza is going to be ordered for lunch. Neither do you need to be bold in fighting over something inconsequential just to show you are in control.

In matters of style, swim with the current.
In matters of principle, stand like a rock.
- Thomas Jefferson

153

You don't have to attend every argument you're invited to.
– Source unknown

Choosing where to be courageous on projects mirrors choosing the right spots for pushing the action in poker. Furthermore, the strategy for deciding fight or flight in projects is much closer to how no-limit poker is played than to limit poker. In limit poker, there is only a moderate amount to be won or lost on a given hand; so if the odds of success are 50/50, you might want to jump in. In no-limit poker, win one big battle and you are positioned to win the war; lose one big battle and you may be out of the game. In business, don't take on a difficult battle unless the decision in question is critical to success and worth putting yourself on the line. Always remember:

Life is a no-limit sport.

Courage to Proactively Engage the Situation

When a courageous decision or act must be taken, don't be a calling station, deferring tough decisions for a later time. Responsibly and courageously, you must initiate encounters at appropriate times. While patience is a virtue, don't wait too long to take courageous action. Remember:

Putting off an easy thing makes it hard.
Putting off a hard thing makes it impossible.
Charles E. Wilson, past President of General Electric

Have a Vision

Start with an ironclad vision of the project. Leading a team that includes peers, customers and others outside of your direct authority means that seniority, job title, and position matter far less than being viewed as the person best able to help the team reach its results. Power, if it should even be called power, flows from the importance of the results themselves, not from some artificial assignment of authority. Therefore, ensure that as a leader, you believe in the vision and can communicate that vision to others.

Taking courageous action for a cause that you don't believe in is very difficult. If you can't communicate the importance of the results to others, in ways they care about, they will not be willing to follow.

A few years ago, I was involved in helping large state agencies put together strategic IT plans. One agency in particular had been struggling for years to get the funding needed for a new computer system. Facilitating a session with the agency leaders, we dragged out a flipchart and wrote at the top of the page the amount of money they needed: $25 million. When asked for their justification for such a large sum of money, their answers consistently boiled down to, "We need a new computer system because the old one is getting older and impossible to maintain."

At that point, I halted the meeting to challenge the group: "If you were in the legislature looking at all possible projects you could fund from the budget, would you vote yes for $25 million to replace another old mainframe system?" Not one of the participants raised their hand in the affirmative – the stated vision simply wasn't compelling. The group then formulated a case that they agreed to, believed in, and could communicate to an external audience. It was true that they needed a new computer system, but the compelling argument and vision for the future was why they needed one. Instead of framing the project in terms of the need for a new computer application, they framed the request in terms of the need for new solutions for enabling citizen self-service, minimizing red tape, and lowering the overall cost of government. Defining the project in terms of credible, business results helped the agency secure the required funding.

Being able to communicate business results that sponsors desire and leaders believe in provides the air cover needed for courageous action. If you can honestly begin every sentence with: "In order to achieve this outcome (e.g. minimizing red tape), I think we should consider the following course of action…" the stakeholders around you will be forced to attack the business problem, not you personally.

Remember the Rules of Engagement

We discussed project values in Chapter 9. Before going on the offensive, you need to have the rules of engagement in place. While it is tempting to justify any and all means necessary to meet the ends, do not charge ahead blindly. Even when everyone agrees perfectly on the goal, stakeholders often strongly disagree on the values and trade-offs that should guide the project in getting there. For example, while in poker we may all agree we want to win money, we may not agree on whether or not it is acceptable to cheat, lie, and steal, or whether or not it is worth the price of staying out too late and underperforming the next day. Written and agreed to project values enable you and the other team members to act independently, while still consistently choosing only the appropriate means for reaching the goals.

Be Emotionally Ready

With the vision and rules of engagement set, the next step is to ensure that you are emotionally ready for battle. When you go on-tilt, allowing emotion to drive poor decision making, you often lose the battle. When it comes time to make a final, difficult decision, typically one participant comes out looking like the calm, rational one focused on results, while another seems to have let their emotion get the better of them. In order to drive high quality decision making and ensure you're not acting on-tilt:

- **Vent beforehand.** Get your emotions out by laughing, crying, cussing, or throwing something. Do whatever you have to do to get it out of your system <u>before</u> you have to make a decision or take action. Humans are emotional creatures and that emotion will come out eventually. It is far better to release the pressure somewhere safe before dealing with other parties in a public setting. Ask a friend to help you become emotionally ready, as discussed in Chapter 8. No matter how important the issue and how strongly you feel about the outcome, you don't want to be like Howard Dean and give others the opportunity to use your passion against you by reframing the discussion away from substantive issues and onto personality.

- **Ensure a business focus, not an ego focus.** Make sure the strategies you pursue are solely focused on efficiently reaching the project's results, rather than being tainted, or overtaken, by an emotional need for revenge, spite, and aggressiveness. Don't take things personally and don't attack others personally.
- **Ensure project values, not personal values, guide your course.** When the going gets tough, it is tempting to fall back on your personal feelings as to the "right" trade-offs between speed vs. cost, getting it right vs. getting it done, or evolution vs. revolution. Project values are agreed to and written down up front in order to regulate this temptation and to create an environment where all stakeholders are responsible for self-enforcing the rules.

By following the three strategies above, odds are you will be more emotionally stable going into a confrontational situation than those around you. Use this to everyone's advantage by stepping forward and helping those around you to vent their emotions appropriately. Otherwise, you are at risk of a situation in which everyone talks past each other because they are overwhelmed by passion.

Never underestimate the importance of emotional readiness in courageous, high quality decision making. As Gerald Weinberg says:

No matter what people say,
it is always a people problem.

To which I would add:

So, the only question is, how much of it is their emotions, and how much of it is yours?

Courage to Find the Underlying Truth

When people are emotional and hostile, hidden within the rhetoric is almost always a kernel of truth. If you can stay calm and positive, you can listen and dig out that truth upon which a better solution can be created. There is nothing more important to establishing positive conflict than being committed to trying to see what the other person sees, but you are missing.

Poker players understand the critical need to try to see what is motivating their opponents' actions. They constantly do the analysis for "putting opponents on a hand." By carefully listening and observing how those around them act, they are able to make an educated guess at what cards are driving their opponent's decision making. Do this well and you win. Do it poorly and you lose.

A good example of putting your opponent on a hand happened to me recently. I was playing against a few friends when three diamonds came on the flop. One of the other players immediately looked at their cards. Before they bet, they looked at their cards two more times. I asked myself, "Why would they need to check their cards three times after the flop?" The obvious answer was: to make sure the cards in their hand were really both diamonds – not hearts. Even though I was holding a pair of jacks, I decided to fold when the other player bet.

On projects, when there is disagreement between passionate stakeholders, try to put the stakeholders on a hand. Ask, "What might they be seeing that I'm not?" Ninety percent of the time, something is making them act the way they are and say the things they say. If you can't put them on one or two probable causes, it is only through getting lucky that you can help them. Putting stakeholders (or poker players) on a hand is a difficult skill but one worth practicing. To get you started, use the following list to help you look beyond the surface discussion to see if the problem might be:

- A disagreement on the relative priorities of the end business results.

- A divergence in opinions on the project values that should be governing the game.
- A conflict between an individual's personal values and the project values.
- An underlying fear that if the project is delivered successfully, it will diminish the stakeholder's ongoing role in the organization.

Courageous Action

Being a calling station is easy – just be a yes man to those around (and especially above) you. Being bold is easy – just bring back the three martini lunch and let the afternoon take you where it may. Being courageous, however, is hard work. Yet, it is worth every ounce of the blood, sweat, and tears you pour into it. To be courageous:

- Set up win-win conflict rather than a chest bumping contest.
- Have the resolve to get to the answers required to deliver the business outcomes for which the organization is counting on you.
- Induce the action by picking your battles wisely and not procrastinating on difficult issues and choices.

Courage is the human virtue that counts most – courage to act on limited knowledge and insufficient evidence. That's all any of us have.
- Robert Frost

BEATING THE ODDS

Like Unbeatable Is Not Unbeatable:
Why Projects Rarely Have Hollywood Endings

*Besides lovemaking and singing in the shower,
there aren't many human activities where there is a
greater difference between a person's self-delusional
ability and actual ability than in poker.*
- Steve Badger, poker professional

You vs. Mel Gibson

We live in the age of instant gratification and personal empowerment. Television programs teach us that any problem, no matter how complex, can be resolved in less than thirty minutes (twenty-two with TiVo). The internet puts the world at our fingertips. We are one-click away from finding anything in the world and having it delivered directly to our doorstep. Current and future healthcare advances promise a pill to correct any and all problems, natural or self-inflicted. Last, but certainly not least, the professional poker on TV is a constant, if subliminal, reminder that with just a little luck, we could all be like Chris Moneymaker and turn a $39 online buy-in into a $2.5 million paycheck at the World Series of Poker.

Against all this, is it any surprise that as project leaders, we often delude ourselves into thinking that we are Hollywood stars capable of Arnold, Demi, and Vin-like heroics, confident we don't have to worry about something as mundane as having a robust, formal, disciplined approach for delivering success? Instead, we can cruise along with full confidence that in the end we will pull off a Hollywood ending.

In the 1994 movie *Maverick*, the protagonist, played by Mel Gibson, had a belief: "Ever since I was a kid, I believed that I had a gift; that if I thought hard enough about a card, I would be able to cut straight to it. Of course, it didn't always work. As a matter of fact it never worked."

Yet, in the movie's climax, when all his chips are in the pot, and it comes down to needing an ace, what appears for our hero? The ace of spades. While this makes for a great blockbuster, I am sorry to break it to you:

**Your project is not a movie,
and you are not Mel Gibson.**

Luck Revisited

Does the fact that we can't will success mean there is no luck that can miraculously or incredulously intervene to make or break your project or tournament? Absolutely not. Of course there is luck involved. At the final table of the 2005 World Series of Poker Event 13, Todd Brunson and Dustin Woolf faced off against each other. Both players, after looking at their hole cards, went all-in. When the cards were flipped, Brunson sat in a powerhouse position: A-A versus A-Q unsuited. Brunson's set-up, having A-A against an ace and a lower, unsuited card, is as dominating a starting position as you can hope for in hold 'em. While not quite unbeatable, it is a 92% favorite to win.

The flop came 10-3-2, with a 5 on the turn, and a 4 on the river. The combination of 2-3-4-5 on the board gave both players the straight (A-2-3-4-5), and they split the pot. For Brunson, this meant that all his patience, discipline, and courage spent waiting for the exact right hand, and getting all of his money into the pot at the mathematically best moment, went for naught. For Woolf, luck had saved the day. The tournament's eventual winner, T.J. Cloutier, reminded the other players at the table that there is no poker karma, no poker justice, and no "poker god" ensuring that the best hand wins on a particular play:

If you think there's any justice in hold'em boys,
you just saw there's not.

What's Your Plan?

You cannot allow yourself to believe that work is like a summer blockbuster where the good guys are destined to win no matter how many unnecessary risks and diversions they take. Just as importantly, you can't fall into the trap of resigning yourself to the belief that the twists and turns of today's complex world negate the importance of strategy and dedication.

Going forward, you have two options: trust your future to chance, leaving it to the turn of a card; or, make your own luck by building a foundation that maximizes your chance of success.

Two Options:
Leave It to Chance or Maximize Success

To maximize success, you must begin the hard work on day-one by anteing up with:
1. Specified Results
2. Adaptable Plans
3. Dedicated Resources
4. A Sufficient Time Span

You must then drive success each and every day by:
5. Focusing on People
6. Practicing Discipline
7. Exercising Courage

There is no talking car to do the driving for you, no Hollywood-style "mission from god" guiding you, no fairy godmother watching over you; the action is totally on you. The deck may seem stacked against you, but you can beat the odds.

Finally,

**The key message of *Beating the Odds* is
<u>not</u> to start treating poker like your job.**

**The key message of *Beating the Odds* is to
ensure you treat your job like a job.**

Virtually every poker book contains the following sentiment: while poker makes a great second job and an even better hobby, it is not a great career choice. My advice is: don't treat poker like a job, don't play just for the money. Play poker to have F-U-N. Take the poker train to New Orleans and stay out all night; get in your car and drive from La Jolla to Vegas and blow it out; qualify on-line for the World Series of Poker and have the experience of a lifetime; play with your friends and shoot the breeze until the sun comes up.

There is plenty of time for patience, hard work, and discipline from nine to five. Just remember to turn it on when you clock in. Because, after all:

Life's more fun when you're winning.

BEATING THE ODDS

APPENDICES

A. Napkin Project Leadership Templates
B. Recommended Reading
C. Driving Success: Project Configurations
D. The Rules of Texas Hold 'em, Hand Ranking, & Poker Glossary
E. Poker Sidebar: *Putting Players on a Hand*

NAPKIN PROJECT LEADERSHIP TEMPLATES

So, you like what you read in the book and are ready to try it at work and at the poker table? Here are six templates to help you give it a try. These templates are also available in a larger format for free download at www.AdvancedStrategies.com/BeatingtheOdds.

Napkin Specified End Results Template

Project Name: _____

Desired Results – The Ends We Are After:
(In terms of outcomes and expressed with the project currency)

_____

_____

Who is Bankrolling the Effort:_____
Are They All-In? ( ) Yes   ( ) No

Napkin Resource Assessment

Project Name:_____

Reviewer:_____

Reviewing the specified results, project plan, and staffing, the current status is as follows:

Each key person assigned to this project:	Red	Yellow	Green
• Has the required knowledge and skills.	O	O	O
• Is available for the time promised.	O	O	O
• Will work well with the team and other stakeholders.	O	O	O

The biggest challenges and obstacles for this project are:

(1): _____

(2): _____

(3): _____

	Red	Yellow	Green
Based on the staffing and other resources, the project is well positioned to overcome the challenges and deliver the specified results.	O	O	O

Napkin Motivating Strategies Template

Project end results:_____

Stakeholder (and Role)	Individual Goal	"Win-win" Motivational Strategy

Napkin Intellectual and Emotional Readiness Template

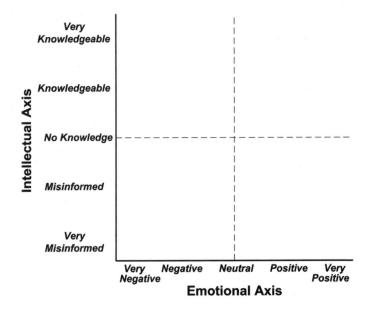

Napkin Project Values Template

Project Values: A House Rules Template	
Low Quality - quick and dirty first steps to get it **done fast.**	**High Quality** – take the opportunity to do it right, even if it **takes longer.**
---♥--------------------♣--------------------◆--------------------♠---	
Low Risk - take a safer and more reliable path even if it **takes longer.**	**High Risk** - accept the risk of short cuts to try and get it **done faster.**
---♥--------------------♣--------------------◆--------------------♠---	
Low Service - don't let customers stand in the way - **deliver faster.**	**High Service** – take a customer first approach even if it causes us to **deliver slower.**
---♥--------------------♣--------------------◆--------------------♠---	
Broad Focus - target is to deliver at least **shallow impacts for everyone.**	**Narrow Focus** – target a specific group to deliver **deep impacts to a small audience.**
---♥--------------------♣--------------------◆--------------------♠---	
Low Comfort - willing to burn out the project team for **higher speed.**	**High Comfort** - must be sustainable for the team, therefore **lower speed.**
---♥--------------------♣--------------------◆--------------------♠---	
Evolution – incremental steps building on existing work with a **higher chance of success.**	**Revolution** – empowered to throw out the old and start fresh with a **lower chance of success.**
---♥--------------------♣--------------------◆--------------------♠---	

Napkin Project Worry Log Template

Sample Napkin Project Worry Log		
#	(1) What I Am Worried About	(2) Strategy for Moving Forward	(3) Immediate Next Steps
1			
2			
...			

RECOMMENDED READING

*I've read dozens of books about heroes and crooks
and learned much from both of their styles.*
Jimmy Buffett, "Son of a Son of a Sailor"

Business Books

The Effective Executive by Peter Drucker
The Secrets of Consulting by Gerald Weinberg
The Cluetrain Manifesto by Rick Levine, Christopher
    Locke, Doc Searls & David Weinberger
All Marketers Are Liars by Seth Godin
Radical Careering by Sally Hogshead
Leading the Revolution by Gary Hamel
Good to Great by Jim Collins
Focus: The Future of Your Company Depends on It by Al Ries
The Price of Government by David Osborne and Peter
    Hutchinson
The End of Advertising As We Know It by Sergio Zyman
Selling the Invisible by Harry Beckwith
Why Decisions Fail by Paul C. Nutt
The 7 Habits of Highly Effective People by Stephen R. Covey

Poker Books

Super System: A Course in Power Poker by Doyle Brunson
The Winner's Guide to Texas Hold'Em Poker by Ken Warren
The Psychology of Poker by Alan N. Schoonmaker, Ph.D.
Play Poker Like the Pros by Phil Hellmuth, Jr.
Poker Wisdom of a Champion by Doyle Brunson

BEATING THE ODDS

DRIVING SUCCESS: PROJECT CONFIGURATIONS

When all four project elements are present (specified results, adaptable plans, dedicated resources, and sufficient time span), the result is a stable platform for moving the project forward, even in rough terrain. When undertakings have less than all four "wheels" adequately in place, some combination of stability, safety and speed is sacrificed as the effort zooms along on only three, two, or even a single wheel. The following four pages analyze the most unstable project configurations:

One Wheelers -
The most unbalanced and slowest moving projects.

Element(s) in Place				Good News! You have a:	Bad News! Symptoms, Risks, and What to Do
Business Result	Adaptable Plan	Dedicated Resource	Sufficient Time Span		
🏍				*Business Objective*	Although you have a goal, it never seems to get accomplished. Specified business results are only the first step. Get this effort off the ground with the plan, resources, and time span required.
	🏍			*Methodology*	You think you know what the next step is but are not sure where you're going. Mobilize a team with business objectives, deadlines, and backed by resources to make the results a reality.
		🏍		*Resource Pool*	You have dedicated resources, but lacking a game plan, the project feels like it is treading water. Drive to success by specifying business objectives, a plan and deadlines.
			🏍	*Deadline*	You have a feeling of panic because the deadline is approaching but you have no way to get there. A deadline is just a deadline until you put a program in place to make it happen.

Two Wheelers -
Tend to be unstable and vulnerable to changes.

Element(s) in Place				Good News! You have a:	Bad News! Symptoms, Risks, and What to Do
Business Result	Adaptable Plan	Dedicated Resource	Sufficient Time Span		
				Goal	Your project team is not in place and you don't have a plan to justify acquiring one. Realize the dream by adding the capacity to make it happen.
				Capacity	Your project team has fallen into being task driven, more focused on the process than the product. Get them refocused on delivering outcomes by giving them a goal of business results and due dates.
				Strategy	Having specified results and a process down on paper looks great, but you are making little progress. Create momentum by applying resources and defining a time span to drive success.
				Momentum	Lacking agreement on specified business results and a plan for delivering those outcomes, your project team is typically running around doing busy-work. Provide a strategy to guide success.

179

Two Wheelers -
Tend to be unstable and vulnerable to changes.

Element(s) in Place				Good News! You have a:	Bad News! Symptoms, Risks, and What to Do
Sufficient Time Span	Dedicated Resource	Adaptable Plan	Business Result		
(bicycle)		(bicycle)		*Schedule*	Your schedule looks great on paper but there is no compelling reason to staff up the project. Determine the desired business results and add a team to deliver.
	(bicycle)		(bicycle)	*Team*	Your team knows what to deliver but is often spinning their wheels in the absence of a schedule. Document their plans and deadlines to get them consistently accelerating toward the goal.

Three Wheelers –

Likely to tip at high speeds, run off the road on challenging corners, and take longer to deliver.

Element(s) in Place				Good News! You have a:	Bad News! Symptoms, Risks, and What to Do
Business Result	Adaptable Plan	Dedicated Resource	Sufficient Time Span		
		●	●	*Ability to Crank Things Out*	Without specified business results, you are probably producing the wrong things (cool technology, shelfware that looks great but no one will ever use, etc). Verify that you have a business target.
●		●	●	*Team with a Deadline*	Your team is working very hard, but often thrashing around, guessing at processes and burning a lot of energy in the absence of a methodology. Give them an adaptable plan – They'll thank you!
●	●		●	*Game Plan*	You have a great game plan but without any players (or other dedicated resources) to take the field, nothing is getting done. Use your game plan to acquire the resources you need.
●	●	●		*Program*	The lack of urgency on your project gives everyone an excuse to work on something else and things grind to a halt. Give your team a finite time span where they can sprint toward success.

181

BEATING THE ODDS

RULES OF TEXAS HOLD 'EM

Overview:

Texas hold 'em is a community card poker game that is typically played with between two and ten people. It is played with a 52 card deck, no wild cards, and no jokers. Each player receives two cards face-down (known as hole cards) and five "community" cards placed face-up in the middle of the table. The objective of the game is to: (1) make the best possible five card poker hand using any combination of hole and community cards; or, (2) to bluff your way to winning the pot.

Betting Structures:

There are four rounds of betting in Texas hold 'em: pre-flop, after the flop, after the turn, and after the river (an explanation of each is given below). There are various betting structures that can be used in Texas hold 'em, depending on whether the game is limit or no-limit and whether there are compulsory bets, commonly known as blinds and antes. A blind is a forced bet made before the cards are dealt to force the action. The explanation below describes a no-limit game with blinds, the style played at the World Series of Poker Championship Event.

Pre-flop:

Before the cards are dealt, the two players to the left of the dealer must post their blinds. The player to the immediate left posts the small blind and the player to his left posts the big blind. All players at the table are then dealt two hole cards. A round of betting then occurs, beginning with the player to the left of the big blind. Players must match at least the amount of the big blind in order to remain in the game. Players also may fold their cards (meaning they are out of the hand) or raise the pot. If there is a raise, all players must call the amount of the raise in order to remain in the hand. Once all players call the last bet, then play moves to the next round.

The Flop:
The dealer turns over three cards in the middle of the table, known as the flop. Another round of betting then occurs, beginning with the player to the left of the dealer. Players can either bet or "check," meaning they pass the bet to the next player. Once a bet is made, players must either call, raise, or fold. Once all players call the last bet, play continues to the next round.

The Turn:
The dealer turns over a fourth community card, known as the turn or fourth street. Another round of betting then occurs, following the sequence used on the flop. Once all players call the last bet, play goes to the next round.

The River:
The dealer turns over the fifth and last community card, known as the river or fifth street. Betting occurs for the last time, following the sequence used on the flop and turn. Once all players call the last bet, they show their cards, starting with the person who bet first on the river. Each player uses their two hole cards, and the five community cards to create their best five card hand. The player with the best hand wins the pot. If multiple players have the same best hand, then they split the pot evenly.

Note: If at any point in the hand all but one of the players fold, then the remaining player automatically wins the hand and does not have to show her cards.

POKER HAND RANKING

(from highest to lowest)

Straight Flush: Five cards of the same suit in sequence (A♥-K♥-Q♥-J♥-10♥)

Four of a Kind: (J-J-J-J-3)

Full House: Three of a kind, plus a pair (K-K-K-Q-Q)

Flush: Five cards of the same suit (♥-♥-♥-♥-♥)

Straight: Five cards of mixed suits in sequence (5-6-7-8-9)

Three of a Kind: (5-5-5-K-2)

Two Pair: (6-6-4-4-2)

Pair: (A-A-6-4-2)

High Card: (A-8-6-4-2)

POKER GLOSSARY

Action: Betting and raising.

All-in: Betting all of your chips.

Ante: Putting money in the pot before the deal. At times, antes are required if the player would like to be dealt cards.

Bad beat: When a big underdog beats a favored hand thanks to a miracle card.

Bet into: Making a proactive and large bet against an opponent who is representing or has a better hand.

Big Blind: The final and largest blind bet.

Blind: A mandatory bet before the deal.

Bluff: Feigning a strong hand and attempting to win the pot by placing a large bet.

Board: The face-up cards in stud or hold 'em.

Bullet: Ace.

Button: A marker used to signify the dealer.

Buy-in: Exchanging money for chips at the start of a game.

Call: Matching a previous bet.

Calling station: A weak player who doesn't raise or fold much.

Cards speak: The rule that the value of a hand is based on what the cards are, rather than what a player declares.

Catch: To be dealt the card you need.

Chase: To stay in the pot against a better hand and against the odds, hoping to get a lucky card.

Check: To pass without betting.

Check raise: To check and then subsequently raise in the same round of betting.

Cowboy: King.

Dead-money: A player who has no realistic chance of winning.

Deal: To distribute the cards to the players. In hold 'em, after every hand the dealer role rotates from player to player clockwise around the table.

Deception: An important and accepted tool of poker.

Doubling-up: Winning an all-in and doubling your chips.

Down cards: Two cards dealt face-down.

Etiquette: The understandings and courtesies of play, of which violations do not constitute cheating.

Fish: An unskilled player who gives money away. "Don't tap the aquarium" because if fishes stop having fun, they will quit donating funds.

Flop: The first three community cards flipped over in hold 'em.

Flush: Five cards of the same suit.

Fold: To surrender a hand by not betting.

Gambler: A player who wagers money against the odds.

Grinding: Playing conservatively to try to use minimal risk to generate modest gains over a long period of time.

Hand: (1) The cards held by a player; or (2) a portion of a game during which all the cards dealt out are played until the pot is won.

Heads-up: (1) A pot that is being contested by only two players; or (2) A game of poker between only two people.

Hold 'em: A seven-card game with two face-down cards for each player and five face-up cards for everyone's use.

Hole cards: Two cards dealt face-down to each player in hold 'em.

Hot streak: A run of good cards and/or luck.

House: The person or organization running a poker game, usually for profit.

House rules: The rules, especially around betting, agreed upon by the players or set by the House.

Inside straight: A broken sequence of four cards, such as 7-8-10-J.

Jacks-or-Better: A form of poker in which a player needs to have at least a pair of jacks to open the betting.

Lay down: To fold a strong hand.

Limit: The maximum bet or raise allowed.

Limit hold 'em: Poker with maximum bets and raises as established by the house.

Limp in: While holding a strong hand, calling rather than raising in the first round of betting.

Luck: Feeling that you are winning or losing more than probability would dictate.

Maniac: A player who does a lot of aggressive raising and bluffing regardless of cards, chips, or position.

Marker: A promissory note like the ones my brother gives me on the back of a pizza coupon.

Monster: A big hand or card.

Muck: To fold.

No-limit hold 'em: A version of hold 'em in which a player may bet any amount of chips (up to the number in front of him) whenever it is his turn to act. A totally different game, and thus strategy, from limit poker.

Nuts: The best possible hand given the cards on the board.

Odds: The chances of getting various hands or of winning.

Offsuit: A hold 'em starting hand with two cards of different suits.

On-tilt: Playing very poorly or wildly because of angry emotion, usually caused by a bad loss.

Open: To start the betting.

Pocket rockets: A pair of aces in the hole.

Poker: A money-management game that uses cards for manipulation and deception for winning. (www.poker.net)

Position: The relative order of betting in regard to other players in the hand.

Pot: The money bet.

Pot limit: Poker stakes in which the maximum bet is equal to the size of the pot.

Raise: To increase the bet.

Raise blind: To raise without looking at your cards.

Re-buy: Taking the option to buy back into a tournament, or to acquire additional chips for hard cash.

Represent: To play as if you hold a certain hand and to communicate that to your opponents.

Re-raise: To raise after having been raised.

River: The fifth and final community card, put out face-up, by itself. Also known as "fifth street" in hold 'em.

Round of betting: The action sequence in which each player is allowed to bet, raise, or fold.

Rush: An emotional high, usually caused by a winning streak.

Second best: The best losing hand, a very dangerous situation.

Selling a hand: A strategy for getting your opponents to call by acting weak.

Set: Three of a kind.

Short-stack: Having a very small number of chips relative to others and/or having the least chips at the table.

Showdown: Showing cards after betting is concluded to determine who wins.

Shuffle: To mix the cards prior to dealing.

Slow play: Checking or otherwise acting weak when you have a strong hand in hope of inducing a bet from your opponent.

Spike: To hit one of the very few cards that can help you (often an ace) on the turn or river.

Split pot: A pot equally divided between two winners (a.k.a. chop the pot).

Stack: A pile of chips.

Stack the deck: Cheat by prearranging the cards for a dishonest deal.

Straight: Five cards in sequence, such as 8-9-10-J-Q.

Streak: A run of winning or losing hands.

String bet: To pause in the midst of betting, accidentally or purposefully to try and get a reaction out of your opponent. This is not allowed in most casinos and poker clubs.

Suited: A hold 'em starting hand in which the two cards are the same suit.

Table stakes: Games in which the betting and raising is limited to the amount of money you have in front of you.

Tells: Characteristics, habits, or actions of a player that give away his hand or intentions.

Texas hold 'em: See hold 'em.

Three of a kind: Three cards of the same value.

Tight player: A player who seldom bets unless he has a very strong hand.

Two pair: Two separate pairs of different values in a hand.

World Series of Poker: Considered by most to be the pre-eminent poker event. It is held annually in Las Vegas and consists of many events including the $10,000 No-Limit Texas Hold 'em World Championship Event.

WSOP: World Series of Poker

POKER SIDEBAR: *Putting Players on a Hand*

In Chapter 11 we talked about the deeper roots of conflict on projects, and the need to strive to understand the issues others view as critical, but that you cannot perceive. This skill is similar to putting a poker player on a hand. By closely following a player's betting patterns and attitude, you can often determine what cards they are holding in their hand. Here are a few tips to help develop this skill at the table:

Strong Is Weak. Although stars such as Ben Affleck, Jennifer Tilly, and Tobey Maguire are occasionally seen at poker tournaments, the majority of poker players you will see are bad actors. This means that a player who comes across as excessively confident or over the top intimidating is likely on a bluff and should be bet out of the hand. Another good clue is to listen to a player's voice. If he shouts out a raise, he is trying to scare everyone away and steal the pot.

Weak Is Strong. If you think most players are bad at acting strong, they are even worse when they feign weakness. Clichéd lines like, "I guess I'll call," or, "I'm just giving my money away on this one," often signal trouble. If a player acts aloof or disinterested in a decent pot, smell danger. After all, what poker player isn't interested in winning a big hand?

Timing Bets. Often, the timing of a bet can tell you more than the amount. If you bet into a player on the flop and he immediately raises you, without giving his hand a thought, chances are he is often on a straight or flush draw. Look for the draw on the board and if it doesn't hit on fourth street, raise again and put him to the test. Another common timing bet is the slow raise on the river, in which a player seems to be deliberating over whether he should call the bet or fold, and after a long time, actually raises. This is a red flag indicating a strong hand. Your opponent is trying to induce betting, so proceed with caution.

BEATING THE ODDS

ACKNOWLEDGEMENTS

Forget about a chip and a chair;
give me a hand and I'll stand.
- Warren Karp, poker pro

This book was created not by me, nor a team, nor a company, but by a network of dedicated professionals across the country. First and foremost, I must thank my brothers for teaching me how to play poker and for encouraging me every step along the way in every way they know how.

Thanks to Christie for playing all of the hardest roles imaginable, from author, to editor, to proofreader, to advisor, to best friend.

Thanks to Sharon for her 24/7 dedication to the book, for her great insights into leading people, and for holding it all together.

Next, thanks to the review team whose input and feedback took a "C-" effort and turned it into something I am glad to have my name on. If you liked a line or thought in this book, it was just as likely to have come from: Craig, Greg, Ila, Matt, Christie, Ed, Sharon, Richard, Charles, Todd, BC, Wes, Wayne, or Catherine as it was from me.

Thanks to the graphics and support team, Laura, Julie, Craig, Mary, and Kuan-hua, without whom the project would have been knocked out early and never recovered.

Thanks to Craig and Marcie for hand holding us through the production process and doing whatever it took to be successful.

Thanks to Cat for always keeping my coffee cup full. Thanks to Jaime for coming through in a pinch.

Thanks to all my friends for whom I have had the pleasure of serving as a consultant, and who have challenged me and made me think hard about what it takes to drive success. I greatly appreciate the opportunities I have had to work with: GPC, SD, DOC, DOH, MISB, MASO, DES, MDA, OSC, DPS, CP, eHEAT, OT, and all the others.

Thanks to Peter Hutchinson. They say when you author your first book you find your voice; I am glad I met you before I found it. Thanks to the authors of *Cluetrain Manifesto*, you saved my life. Thanks to Gene Mrozinski for helping me articulate my thinking on the essential elements of project management and leadership.

Thanks to Deering and Down for showing me what it takes to create something and for giving me a copy of *American Friend* when I needed both a friend and a rockin' soundtrack to keep me going through the night.

Thanks to SSSSSSsssssssssssss for taking care of Z, teaching me how to win, and giving me the love and support needed to have the confidence to get through this.

Thanks to my dad for teaching me how to study the odds and gamble smart, and to Barb and Wayne for teaching me how to place the big bets.

Finally, and most importantly, thanks to Abe, Richard and everyone at Advanced Strategies, who are the true authors of this book. Thanks for taking eighteen years to figure all this out, and eight years of teaching me how to make it practical. While this book is my autobiography, it is your life story. Again, thank you Strategists: Richard, Abe, Farrell, Karen, Gail, Jerry, Sharon, Ed, Kahil, Clowse, Greg, Craig, Christie, Ila, Gino, Charles, Mary, Fran, Colleen, Kuan-hua, and everybody else.

I hope you enjoy it.

BEATING THE ODDS: *The Live Experience*

One of the most widely attended and most highly rated leadership presentations in the 23 year history of the conference.
- Rich Spencer, Project Leader, Minnesota IT Symposium

Sit & Go: An energetic and entertaining, 60-minute motivational talk targeted to large teams needing to transform how they approach leadership. The one-hour speech emphasizes:
1. Specifying desired business results and using those results to drive decision making and actions.
2. Taking the time to understand what motivates people using a problem-solving based approach.
3. Having the courage to make the tough choices required to deliver success.

Multi-table: A two day, hands-on course combining lectures and exercises to assist students in:
- Understanding the seven fundamental strategies critical for establishing and leading successful projects in today's world.
- Practicing the techniques in a series of live exercises, so students are prepared to walk out and begin applying them in their day-to-day activities.

Single-table: From two to ten days, this intimate, hands-on series goes beyond helping students understand the concepts and into developing the dexterity needed to confidently apply them on large, complex projects. This facilitator driven course is limited to 16 students and is targeted to those who are betting their careers on the ability to successfully lead projects in political and chaotic environments.

These courses are available in both poker and non-poker formats.

For more information, contact me at:
jschroeder@advstr.com or 770-936-4000.